Creative Humor at Work

Living the Humor Perspective

Sandra S. Meggert

University Press of America,® Inc.
Lanham · Boulder · New York · Toronto · Plymouth, UK

Copyright © 2009 by
University Press of America,® Inc.
4501 Forbes Boulevard
Suite 200
Lanham, Maryland 20706
UPA Acquisitions Department (301) 459-3366

Estover Road
Plymouth PL6 7PY
United Kingdom

Library of Congress Control Number: 2008936382
ISBN-13: 978-0-7618-4361-0 (paperback : alk. paper)
ISBN-10: 0-7618-4361-2 (paperback : alk. paper)
eISBN-13: 978-0-7618-4362-7
eISBN-10: 0-7618-4362-0

Dedicated to my father, Erich, who modeled using humor appropriately and to my three brothers, Ken, Sandy, and Ed who made sure I used it.

Table of Contents

Foreword

Few periods in our nation's history have posed so many challenges, both personal and environmental, for young and old alike. On a daily basis, we are faced with problems and decisions that must be made for which there are often no easy, or even clear, choices. Therefore, it should not be surprising that people seek whatever remedies that present themselves, including the magical quick fixes promoted by the purveyors of programs and products that promise worry-free remedies that require little effort on the part of the user.

It is in this environment that there has been a new appreciation of the broadband positive effects of the use of humor both as a remedy itself as well as a tool to be blended with other solution-focused counseling interventions. It can bring a better sense of well being to the individual who uses it and can increase one's ability to cope with a variety of difficult, challenging situations.

This book is in the forefront of an emerging recognition of the power of humor to aid not only practicing counselors and caregivers, but also their clients in coping with the difficult situations they face. In this book, you will find a storehouse of useful ideas and resources for the use of humor by persons in many walks of life.

I strongly recommend this book as one that will be a joy to anyone who reads it as well as a source of highly useful interventions that you can use in your work. Sandi Meggert has been a longtime proponent of the use of humor in counseling and life. Through workshops and conferences, she has both modeled and taught us all how to use humor effectively. Read it and use the ideas it presents. You will smile and laugh often—as will those with whom you come into contact.

Garry R. Walz, Ph.D.
Professor Emeritus, The University of Michigan

Preface

Much of the information contained in this book has been gathered from interactions and experiences over a period of twenty years during the presentation of my "Creative Humor at Work" seminars. All of the stories and anecdotes are true stories, many told by participants during the seminars or friends who acknowledged my SOS for funny stories. The stories are used to demonstrate the principles contained in the seminar, primarily, learning to look at life situations from a humor perspective and experiencing the benefits.

The purpose of the "Creative Humor at Work" seminar is to teach people how to create more laughter in their lives. In the early 80s at a professional conference, another participant and I decided we wanted to sing after the evening meal. As we started singing, others joined in and soon most of the group was involved. Those who did not want to sing left and those who remained were laughing and smiling. Later that evening, in a discussion with a colleague, it struck me that while we were singing I saw a side of this group I had never seen at these meetings. As I expressed this, my colleague offered me the opportunity to plan next year's dinner entertainment. Instead, at the next annual conference another colleague and I presented a program on play. It was scheduled at the end of day and out of over 100 people at the conference, 80 were in our session. That response seemed to support my observation that, too frequently, many of us tend to take ourselves too seriously. About the same time, I attended two workshops, "The Healing Power of Laughter and Play" and Joel Goodman's "Laughter and Creativity." Shortly afterwards, a professional colleague and I created the first "Creative Humor at Work" seminar to demonstrate the power of laughter and how it can help to alleviate stress. Since humor and laughter are thought to stimulate the body's production of endorphin, we also created our concept of what an endorphin looks like and named him "Dorph." Dorph and, later on, his friend Dorfi participated in all of those early seminars. Dorph was designed to make people smile.

We began doing these seminars for counseling organizations in the United States and in Europe. Since the mid 80s, I have expanded my presentations into health organizations, businesses, and college and university staffs throughout the United States and in Europe. After doing my most recent two-day seminar in

Germany, I was welcomed by several "graduates" of previous seminars who regaled me with stories of what they had learned and how they continue to apply these humor principles. Some of these people had attended the seminar ten years ago!

This book's format follows the structure of the seminar with some embellishments that could not be included in short workshops. One addition includes applications of the *Humor Perspective*. Humor is applicable in most settings and I chose examples of using humor in illness, non-custodial parental communication at a distance, war, corporate offices, virtual teams, and in counseling relationships. In the 1980s using humor focused on health care and health care settings, and my example is of a current terminal patient rather than the health care staff, a little different perspective but for a similar purpose. Little has been written about long-distance, non-custodial parental relationships with their children. What there is stresses the importance of communication. My case example describes how humor enhanced that communication. In the last twenty years, humor in office settings has been more and more acceptable, and many humorists focus on seminars and workshops in that arena so a brief discussion of creating humor at the office is included. Office structures have changed and team members are not always in close proximity which makes it more difficult to establish comfortable team relations. For that reason, a short discussion of virtual teams and one person's method of using humor to build the team is incorporated. Lastly, I have been asked many times to teach people how to use humor in counseling relationships. I do not think I can do that. However, what I can do is give guidelines and cues, similar to what we teach counselors to do anyway and that is part of the segment on humor in counseling.

For purposes of this book, the definition of laughter is the physical response to something that is funny and it is stimulated by humor.

Acknowledgements

My thanks go to three friends who took time to edit the manuscript, Monty Renfro, Renny Greenmun, and Cherie Renfrew-Starry, as well as Seow Ling Chua, who both edited and formatted the final draft. Thanks also to the friends who provided the stories used to illustrate the concepts.

Chapter 1

Introduction to the *Humor Perspective*—
What is it?

Scenario 1. You are having a bad day. Your alarm clock did not go off and it was lucky you woke up when you did. You do not have time to grab breakfast and have to rush out the door. A garbage truck blocking your driveway further delays you and then you have to follow it slowly up the hill. With the traffic as congested as it usually is, it will be a miracle for you to get to your workshop on time. As you drive along, you are mentally plotting dire consequences for everyone who is not traveling as fast as you would want. You arrive at your destination, feeling harried and in a sour mood.

Scenario 2. You are having a bad day. As you drive, you consciously decide not to seek revenge on the drivers who are slowing you down and instead take notice of the scenery around you. As you approach the Carnation plant, over the top of an adjacent two-story building, you can see part of a billboard. It says, "Employee of the Month." As you get closer, you see the rest of the sign. It is a picture of a Guernsey cow. You chuckle and suddenly the day seems not quite so bad. You arrive at the hotel where your meeting is being held, see an empty parking place right in front and hurry to get there first. As you are turning into the space, you read the sign, "Employee of the Month," and the space is empty! You walk into the workshop with a smile. What happened?

It is simple. In the first scenario you wanted to punish the whole world for your bad feelings. In the second you chose to look around, shift your focus off your frustration and, in the process, you found some of the absurdity out there and were willing to laugh. Basically, you made a different choice. You chose the *Humor Perspective*. Electing to utilize a different perspective is akin to solving crossword puzzles. There is a clue, and the solver must consider various definitions for that clue, identify words adjacent to the missing one, and see which word fits. In other words, the puzzle solver looks at different perspectives to find the answer. Life offers us the same puzzle, and we can consciously look for what is funny or absurd, thereby creating our own mirth and realizing some of the benefits of a good laugh which are helpful in helping us lighten up.

As we grow up, life becomes more serious. Many of us put on a serious face as we leave our childhood behind. Life is not always fun. We encounter many situations that are not funny and give us little, if any, desire to smile or laugh. Even if we were fortunate enough to have had a childhood where we were encouraged to laugh, play, and be creative, these experiences do not appear to make it inevitable that we adopt a *Humor Perspective* as adults. We still have to accept the belief that it is possible to be playful even when we are involved in serious tasks. My "Creative Humor at Work" seminar was designed to nurture our playful sides and help us find and create more humor in our lives, to learn to look at life from a *Humor Perspective*.

The philosophy underlying "Creative Humor at Work" is that in any situation in which we find ourselves, we have choices as to how to react. We can feel angry, sad, frustrated, and stressed, or we can try to find the humor in the situation and smile. Loss of a friend, a job, or good health are not funny, so we may have to look at ourselves and our reactions to these events to find the humor. In many cases, we *are* what is funny! If only we could see ourselves in this way. Humor is often found in the way we approach or behave in uncomfortable situations. However, generally we are too trapped in our own egos to appreciate our own absurdities. One way to look at ourselves during such times is to adopt a *Humor Perspective* and actively seek out the humor or absurdity of our behavior. Have you ever found yourself talking louder when communicating with someone who cannot hear and who "listens" by reading lips? One *Saturday Night Live* skit said it was including adaptations for the hearing impaired. The modification was a talking head at the bottom of the screen that yelled everything the actors were saying, a way of exaggerating a frequent reaction of hearing persons who have had little or no experience with communicating with non-hearing persons. This same phenomenon often occurs when talking with someone who is speaking in a foreign language.

Laurel, a friend and a seminar participant, demonstrated the use of the *Humor Perspective* with the following story. She was hydroplaning on a choppy lake with her father and their dog, which was sitting in the front of the boat. It was so rough that there were no other boats on the lake. As they returned to the dock, feeling smug about being successful at hydroplaning under adverse conditions, the dog jumped onto the dock just before a big wave hit, swamping the boat. It sank right next to dock. She and her father, both in the water, laughed uproariously as the dry dog watched them from the dock. Laurel was still laughing as she retold this story that happened twenty years ago. This points out another advantage: a good laugh lasts for years, perhaps even a lifetime.

Lightening up can help us realize the cost of worrying about situations that cannot be changed is emotionally draining and not worth the effort. Sometimes we need help in doing this. Several years ago I wrecked my car. The day after the accident I was obsessing about the fact that I should have stayed overnight in Tulsa, when I was too tired to drive another three hours to my destination. After listening awhile, my friend noted, "I understand. You had been on an airplane for ten hours and were in a hurry to get home so you could crash. You just did it early!" We laughed and I realized we often feel stressed or worried about what is past or what is in the future as well as things over which we have no control. At that moment, the laughter served to bring me back to the present to focus on the reality, which was that I could not undo anything but I could solve the problem of repairing my car. Finding humor in the situation unlocked my ability to proceed constructively instead of dwelling on the past.

Another time, upon landing in Houston en route to Corpus Christi, I found my flight had been cancelled. It was about 2:30 pm and I was scheduled to make a keynote speech at nine the next morning so I had the time to standby for the flights starting at 5:30pm until 10:30pm. I decided to call my contact at the hotel, but when I dialed 411 for information on my cell phone, a light flashed and the telephone went dark, so I went to a pay phone and dialed 411. Nothing happened. I called the operator to ask how I could get to information and an automated voice told me to listen to the instructions. There was silence and then a dial tone. I tried again, and a real person told me to dial 1-411. I did and heard the automated operator say, "Please deposit fifty cents." I did and got the number. Information printed on the front of the telephone said, "Fifty cents to call anywhere in the United States" and I only had two more quarters when I dialed the hotel. I received the message, "Please deposit fifty cents for the first two minutes." I thought the call might take longer than two minutes and as there was a credit card slot, I swiped my credit card and received the same message as before. After three such messages, I deposited my last two quarters. The message then was, "You are using too many forms of payment, goodbye." I started to laugh and, since my two quarters were returned, I decided I would just have to talk fast and repeated my call. I said what I had to say and a recorded message came back with, "Please deposit fifty cents for two minutes." I hung up. I finally found a seat in the crowded terminal and then realized I would need more quarters to make another call. Rather than give up my seat, I decided to ask the gentleman sitting next to me if he had change for one dollar. He said no but that he had two quarters and gave them to me. As I was reaching for my wallet, he said, "No, I don't like to carry change in my pocket, you are doing me a favor" and gave me another penny. When his friend returned, he asked him if he had quarters for me. The friend said yes and gave me four quarters and assorted small change. I went to my wallet and found I did not have a dollar bill and tried to give the money back to him. He said, "No, I don't like to carry change in my pocket going through security so you are doing me a favor." So now I had "helped out" two people!

I finally arrived at Corpus Christi and was walking to the taxi stand when I saw a van to my hotel. There was a flight crew inside. I sat next to the flight attendant and asked where they were coming from. She said, "Houston. I was your flight attendant." So much for my observation skills! I commented that her hair had been different, and we both chuckled. When I checked in at the hotel, the desk clerk told me I had had a reservation for the night before. I told him it should have been for now and asked when the conference had started. He said, "Today." I thought I had missed my keynote! After questioning everyone I encountered to see if they there for the conference to no avail, I met three women and their children on the elevator. I asked them about the conference and they confirmed that the conference had indeed started that day. "What happened?" I queried. "Not much," one of the women replied. "What about tomorrow?" I asked. Another woman said, "Oh, we have a keynote speaker and workshops." My response was, "Thank goodness. I am the keynote speaker, and I thought I had missed the convention." We all laughed and I happily went on my way.

At each point in this long story, I could have been frustrated or felt stressed but instead chose to look at the events as an adventure, using the *Humor Perspective* and ultimately I used the story as an introduction to my speech. Afterward, a woman came rushing up to me and said she was a friend of the woman in the elevator who had eased my mind and said she had heard the story from her the night before and added that they had all laughed heartily.

There are three rules in learning to view the world through a *Humor Perspective*. Rule One: Choose to look for humor in a situation; Rule Two: Recognize that it needs to be funny only to you; and, Rule Three: Realize you do not have to share it with anyone. Rules One and Two can be effectively used whether we are alone or in a group. Rule Three comes into play when we are interacting with others.

Rule One: Choose to Look for Humor

Choosing to see humor in a situation is critical, particularly in the beginning while we are learning the *Humor Perspective*. It takes an active choice to distance ourselves from unpleasant emotions and examine the situation to see what is funny. This takes skill and practice, and there are frequent examples in this book demonstrating this skill. Stepping back to look at a situation differently allows us some distance from the problem, a time out. Frequently, during this brief respite, we become aware of different aspects of the situation that were initially unnoticed. Through this means, when we focus back on the situation, it seems to have magically changed. The situation is actually still the same as it was. Our perception is the altered ingredient. Making the choice to seek humor or absurdity can be difficult because on first observation no humor may be evident. Sometimes, it takes diligence, effort and persistence to find it.

Rule Two: It Only has to be Funny to Me

The second rule is that we must realize that each of us has a unique appreciation of what is funny and each of us laughs at different things. Humor is an attitude we develop about contradictions in our world. When we encounter what we think is funny, we react with a smile or laughter. When we search out and appreciate humor in our world, a paradox occurs. We expect others to laugh at the same things we do. When using the *Humor Perspective*, we are helping ourselves. If we think something is funny, then it is . . . to us and that is all that is needed.

Rule Three: I Do Not Have to Share It

We erroneously conclude, at times, that it is *necessary* for others to laugh at the same things we do. This attitude puts pressure on us to entertain, and we lose the benefit of spontaneity and enjoyment of our own sense of the absurd. Consequently, Rule Three says we do not have to share our funny observations with anyone. We can, of course, and others might laugh . . . or maybe they will not. When humor is shared, there is an element of risk involved. As we practice the *Humor Perspective*, we will become more sensitive to humor and absurdity in the world. We will become more aware of how others respond and what makes them laugh, and will be able to judge better whether our perception will be appreciated. This awareness takes away or diminishes some of the risk inherent in sharing humor. We can create a *Humor Kit* in our mind, where we store many of the things that we think are funny, and remember them in times of stress.

Current opinions vary as to whether laughter and humor impact physical health, but those of us who do humor seminars and workshops believe this to be true. There is more and more research available to support the premise that humor is a valuable tool for keeping us physically and mentally healthy (Coleman, 2005; Mahony, 2000; McGhee, 1999; Mauger, 2001; Wilson, 1999). The topic of humor is frequently discussed in the media. The January 2005 issue of *Time* magazine devoted a major segment of one issue to the topic of "Mind & Body Happiness" (pp. A1–A68) and identified laughter as one sign of happiness. Humor experts have their own Internet web sites, and humor consulting has become a legitimate business. Backed by opinions about the impact humor and the resulting laughter have on our bodies, the teaching of how to use humor as a tool to use in daily activities has become a recognized profession. Using a variety of beliefs and philosophies about the objectives of such instruction, these humorists strive to help people lighten up.

In learning about the *Humor Perspective*, it is important that we become cognizant of the positive effects of constructive humor. Seeking humor becomes a practical method to help us feel less stressed and focused on the positive. Klein (1989) coined the term *mirthmyopia* to describe what he called our "greatest disease." He noted, "We get so caught up in our everyday struggles that we forget to step back and see the comic absurdity of some of our actions" (p. 13). Adopting a *Humor Perspective* and making a deliberate choice to look for humor in situations enables us to cope better with life's challenges. Although laughing may not make the problem go away, it does make everything feel better for a short while. Many of us already know about psychological, physical, and social benefits of laughter, humor, and positive attitudes. Several of these benefits will be described in detail later in the book.

Although most of us do think humor and laughter are beneficial, we forget to search for humor in our personal situations and, consequently, tend to store negative emotions. When we use the *Humor Perspective*, we are able to experience the benefits of laughter which are often cathartic. Perhaps the essence of this is that we must develop a belief or expectation that we *will* encounter absurdity and incongruities in our daily lives. Reality is that if we expect to find humor, we find it . . . but often we stop looking short of discovering anything funny.

Many of us have barriers, real or imagined, that prevent us from utilizing the humor around us to alleviate stress or to adopt the *Humor Perspective*. In this book, several obstacles will be described, barriers that prevent us from using humor or even recognizing that something is funny. Then, once we have understood and overcome our reticence to be actively funny and decide to adopt the *Humor Perspective* and look for the funny side and the incongruities in our environment, we need to understand some important differences between constructive and destructive humor, what is appropriate and what is not. Sometimes we find ourselves in situations where we can see the humor but pointing it out might be hurtful to someone, while other times, remarking about an aspect of what we are experiencing can be positive and stimulate beneficial interactions. All of us need to know the difference so we can utilize humor in a positive and functional manner.

Another component of the *Humor Perspective* is to recognize that men and women often respond to different types of humor. We learn about what is proper for males and females in our own cultures. We all belong to many cultures. In any group to which we belong, each role we fill is part of a culture and has expectations that we must learn in order to participate successfully within that culture. Our family is one example of a culture and many of the lessons learned in our family, whether explicit or implicit, stay with us over our lifetime. This is also true when applied to the use of humor because we receive messages about using humor in our family as well. With this in mind, gender differences both in appreciation and expression of humor are explored in this book.

Since humor is often a significant part of relationships, a discussion of humor in relationships is included. The relationship model identifies ways that humor can be used at the various stages of an ongoing involvement with a significant other. As a relationship develops and the individuals get to know each other better, there are subtle changes in humor that frequently reflect shifts in the intimacy of knowing. Through longevity of relationships, we learn what is acceptable and what is not as a focus of joking. We learn to predict what will work and what will not. We learn how to make our partner more comfortable by being funny and conversely, how to make our partner uncomfortable with our levity.

Continuing in our quest to learn about and adopt the *Humor Perspective*, another chapter is devoted to specific "humor skills" that can be learned and applied in stressful situations. These are identified and some methods to learn them are described. These skills include: laughing at ourselves, creating metaphors, verbal caricatures and puns. An additional segment describes humor stretches and magic which frequently include laughing at yourself.

Additional chapters include applications of humor with specific populations: individuals with severe illness and their caretakers, parents who maintain long distance communications with their non-custodial children, and a soldier deployed in Iraq. A chapter discussing humor in the workplace suggests usage of humor in office environments, in working with virtual teams, and in counseling relationships. And, finally, appendices contain methods, resources, and Internet contributions that can help build your Humor Kit, the humor you store in your head and bring out during stressful situations to distract yourself.

Chapter 2

Benefits of Humor

Most of us believe laughter is good for us. We may not have thought about why. We just know we feel better after a good laugh. "Humor, particularly when it is accompanied by laughter, promotes physiological, psychological and social change" (Myers, Sweeney, Witmer, 2000, p. 254). Contentions about the benefits of humor, laughter, and positive attitudes have sparked extensive scientific interest in recent years. Sultanoff (1999) has questioned claims regarding its benefits and the limitations of such research, and he has expressed his concern about the few existing experimental studies and their conflicting results. He agrees we do know about the physiological impacts of laughter; however, he raises questions about the nature of biochemical changes and their impact on health and wellness. He identifies three "facts" that humor presenters identify: "Children laugh 400 times a day while adults laugh 15 times. Endorphins, the body's natural pain killers, are released during deep heartfelt laughter" and immunoglobulin A (an antibody), killer T-cells and tolerance to pain "are increased with laughter while serum cortisol (a hormone secreted when one is under stress) is decreased with laughter" (p. 1). He proceeds to debunk each claim as not supportable by adequate research and conclusive scientific evidence. On the other hand, Berk and Tan at Loma Linda University (1999) have conducted controlled scientific experiments that have proven those early results. They found first of all that laughter increases the immune system's activity in this way:

- Natural killer cells (the cells that attack virus and tumor cells) increase in number and activity.
- More T cells (which wait to be told to do something) are activated than normal.
- The antibody immunoglobulin A (which protects the upper respiratory tract) increases.

- Gamma interferon increases. This cytokine tells different components of the immune system to turn on.
- Immunoglobulin G (the immunoglobulin produced in the greatest quantity) and Complement 3 (which helps antibodies pierce dysfunctional or infected cells) increase both during laughter and the next day.

The research also showed that in general, stress hormones—which actually constrict blood vessels and suppress immune activity—decrease in the body as a result of laughter" (Berk & Tan, 1999, p. 1).

While opinions vary about the comprehensiveness and adequacy of current research, this does not necessarily disprove the positive impact of humor, laughter, and positive feelings on our lives. Berk and Tan view the study of humor as a legitimate science and plan to do further research to expand the knowledge of "psychoneuroimmunology and the mechanism linkage modulation between anticipatory positive behaviors and neuroendocrine and immune responses" (Berk & Tan, 2006, Next Steps section). This chapter describes some of the better known and proven benefits of laughter and positive attitudes.

The benefits of laughter can be categorized into three areas: social, physical, and psychological. Social benefits are those involving responses when interacting with other people; physical benefits involve physiological changes within one's body; and psychological benefits result from a shift in focus from the negative thoughts, feelings, or perceptions to the positive.

Social Benefits

Adler (1957) believes that each of us has a basic need to belong, to feel part of a group. William Glasser (1965) maintains that a fundamental human need is to love and be loved. If either of these theorists is right, and there are a significant number of people who agree with them, then methods for linking people, for helping them come together with others is a significant life task. The use of humor is one means of accomplishing this goal.

Provine (in Parmar, 2005) describes laughter as a communication tool that is primarily used interpersonally since it occurs more frequently in social situations than in solitary situations. He explains it is hard "to tell yourself a joke and convincingly respond, 'No, no, I really hadn't heard that one before.'" (p. A5) When people are interacting socially, their laughter often brings connections with others and becomes infectious. Consider a time when something tickled you. When you laughed, what did the people around you do? Did they laugh also? Even when they do not know why, people often join in. There are times you might not think it appropriate to laugh aloud, and you might have struggled not to do so. As part of this effort, you may have made a snorting sound. Eventually someone sitting near you turned to you and may have responded in a similar manner also struggling not to laugh and eventually you both "lost it." Or, if someone genuinely laughed, what did you do? A perfect example of this was a segment on the *Mary Tyler Moore Show* (Brooks & Burns, 1992). Lou, the producer, and Murray, the writer, were in Lou's office laughing at a comment Murray had made about the death of Chuckles the Clown when Ted, the pompous newscaster, walked in. He had no idea what this was about but soon Ted was laughing almost as hard as the other two. In this case, the laughter provided distance from pain of losing a friend, even if Ted did not know this, and became contagious. When we hear genuine laughter, it is hard not to join in. Another example: notice what happens if a small child laughs. Spectators may or may not laugh aloud but will at least smile. It is very hard to resist a child's expression of joy or delight.

Laughter is attractive and brings people together in an almost magnetic way. How often do you choose to spend time with someone who is grouchy all of the time? If you are like most people, your response is likely to be, "As little as possible!" Consider individuals in your life. As you remember these people, what characteristics stand out for you? For most of us, a sense of humor is part of an internal list of desirable behaviors in others. If someone in your life is to describe you, would a sense of humor be part of that description? Do you think you are perceived as smiling or laughing frequently? Do you have a person in your life who can serve as a role model for using humor? Examine how this individual responds to others. What can you learn from this person?

Another perspective about the social attractiveness of laughter is that it creates connections between people. Tom, a Presbyterian minister, tells his story about how humor saved his life:

> I was part of a two-week mission trip to Heredia, Costa Rica, with twenty-five high school students, and my brother helping a very poor village build a four room home for their pastor, which would also double as the local church. The work was difficult and demanding as we needed to haul 50-pound bags of cement down a 35-foot steep mountain, sometimes in the rain of the afternoon, mix the cement in a shallow hole in the ground with shovels, and then transport the cement by wheel barrow to the foundation. I was also preaching and leading worship services at night, so on the bus ride home I would prepare my talks. At the weekend break between the two weeks, I decided to stay behind and not go with the team into town, and instead I was to work on my sermons for the coming week. There was a beautiful large tree near the dining hall, and I so wanted to read and write and pray there. I waved goodbye to the bus load of students and adult sponsors and my brother, and headed back to our cabana for my Bible and papers.

> As I walked into our little cabin, I heard noises coming from our bedrooms and I announced myself to who I thought were camp workers fixing our shower that had broken a couple of days before, when out of one of our rooms burst a young man with a .38 revolver and he pointed it to my forehead and shouted at me in Spanish to lay down on the floor. I had a feeling that getting on the floor was not a good idea, so I sat on the sofa and said with serious tones, "Soy del pastor, soy del pastor" (I am a pastor). He lowered the gun from my head,

breathed in a heavy sigh, and tapped my chin with the gun, to raise my head so he could look at me. As I raised my head, and our eyes met, he smiled at me, and we connected in a strange way, a way that I knew he was not a harmful person. At that moment, another young man, very short and angry, jumped into the room screaming at the top of his lungs, "Plata! Plata! Plata! Donde esta la Plata!" I am confident that in moments of high stress, your brain does not function well in another language and I reasonably translated Plata, as plates. When I figured out what they wanted in my mind, I was thrilled to help these gentlemen. So, I raised my hand to speak, as if I was in a level one class on criminal behavior and I needed to interrupt the teacher with the answer. So, I told them I knew where the plata was (just in the kitchen behind me) and I convinced the one young man with whom I had made a connection and who still had the gun, to allow me to get up and proceed with caution, my arms raised in submission, into the kitchen to retrieve the plates. When I came around the corner with a stack of plastic plates, the young man with the gun tried desperately to keep himself from laughing, and the more he tried not to laugh, the sillier it became, and the funnier it tickled him. I was so pleased with myself that I put my arm on the shoulder of the young man with the gun, who was now laughing hysterically, and handed the plates to the other person who was not very happy at all. He threw the plates on the floor, and with a terribly patronizing tone and poor attitude he said, "Plata, plata es dinero, dolares, stupido" which roughly translated means plata is slang for money, and is translated as silver, and I was simply an idiot.

Unfortunately my joy turned to fear, and I sat on the sofa with my head in my hands. They returned to our rooms and took what they wanted. As they left through the back bedroom, breaking out a window and into the yard, I turned to see where they were going. The young man without a sense of humor grabbed the revolver, pointed it at me, and the other kinder young man reached for his arm and pushed the gun down just as he fired. The bullet ricocheted off the door handle and went into the floor between my feet. I remember it being very quiet for what felt like a long time. Then I ran through the front door yelling for the camp custodians, who came running with machetes to my rescue, and as we were all running and hollering I kept thinking of that strange connection with the thief, the smile and laughter we shared, the touch, and I had to stop for a moment beneath the tree near the dining hall, and I laughed until I cried until I laughed again. And I said a prayer of thanksgiving, and then I called my wife. Funniest part of all is what they took. They stole all of my underwear and all of the other men's underwear from their suitcases. I almost lost my life over my underwear?! Several hours later, as I was telling the story with passion and intensity, my brother leaned over to me and said with a Mexican accent, "Senor, did you know that these men were the notorious Banditos de la Fruita de Looma?"

Humor is powerful. Each relationship and each group has its own acceptable brand of humor which can control behavior by being used in either constructive or destructive ways. Humor and laughter create cohesion in a group and allow people to become part of the group, or, conversely, they can be used to exclude people. In this next case, humor was used as a coping mechanism for living and protecting the sanctity of the family. A close friend confided:

> I've often reflected on how my upbringing taught me to use humor as a means (the only means) for coping with the harsher realities of life. When I was growing up, our family was desperately poor and my father was an alcoholic—two hardships which bolstered one another. Although there was much in our circumstances that encouraged dissatisfaction, our parents, through perfectly sustained example, instilled in us, their children, the unspoken but inflexible rule that we were never to whine or complain or cry about anything we were unhappy with. We were, however, allowed to laugh at our problems. What this meant was that there was no disappointment, no hurt, no fear that was too painful to be talked about—as long as we were poking fun of it. If Daddy got drunk and fell down the steps last night or if we had to wonder where we would go if we couldn't scrape up the rent this month—those things we could describe as enormously funny. Of course, at bottom, everyone understood that the joke was no joke.

> My friend observed that Henry Adams once said, "The family mind approaches unity more nearly than is given to most works of God," and when my mother was dying from cancer, I came to appreciate our family's strange (to others, maybe) use of humor and how it both unifies and comforts us. Initially, I took care of my mother by myself and will always be grateful for the support and sympathy of my nearby friends. Yet even now, thirty years later, I can remember the powerful emotional release I felt when my two sisters arrived and the three of us went to the hospital to wait outside Mother's room. There, we were able to
> laugh at the fact that our beloved mother was dying and there was nothing we could do about it other than, possibly, to find her second (ex) husband and unload her on him. There, we were able to laugh at the fact that she had no insurance other than an accident policy and that there was no outside money to pay the hospital bills, so we could picture putting her in a car and letting it roll down a hill. I never could have expressed such preposterous ideas to my loving and supportive friends because, I fear, they would not have understood that the joke was no joke. They would not have known that a joke was code for "I hurt." (MR, personal communication, August 2006)

Fine (cited in Stambor, 2006) believes groups have "referential in-jokes" (p. 60) to indicate they belong and the members use these to test potential members to see if they match up with group norms. There is an often-repeated story about men who had been together in prison for many years and who had retold the same jokes over and over. As the years passed, they all knew every word to every joke so they only said the number of that joke and every one would have a good laugh. A new prisoner observed someone yelling a number and everyone responding with laughter. After several such incidents and wanting to fit in, the new person yelled out, "Number eight." No one laughed. He yelled out another number, same reaction. He asked his cellmate about this. The response was, "Some people just don't know how to tell a joke." Have you ever been in a group that had "inside" jokes? How did you respond? How long did it take for you to become part of that inside group? How did you accomplish that?

In addition, group members can be manipulated into laughing at or poking fun of someone else in order to be accepted by the group and/or to prove allegiance to the group. Think of a group to which you have belonged or you have observed. Was there someone who always seemed to be the focus of jokes, someone who was being laughed at, not with? Of course, that person may have laughed as well, whether it was comfortable or not. Did you think the focus person enjoyed the attention or did that individual's laugh sound less than genuine? If the group was attractive or important to that person, the individual conformed by responding in the expected way—by laughing or at least pretending to do so.

While humor can force members to conform to group norms, it can also identify problems in a group. In groups that have been together over a long period of time, established overt and covert norms or rules dictate how issues in the group are resolved. If the level of trust is not such that conflict resolution takes place, the resulting issues and feelings will be evident in the humor that ensues. In such a group, listen to the topic of the humor and the relevant, unresolved issues will be obvious. People tend to joke about issues that are unresolved or bothersome. This does not mean that humor will resolve issues, just that it is often used to cover up or be indirect about dissentions. Sarcasm is often the method used. The most successful (funny) sarcasm seems to come from people who are a step removed from the conflict, not directly involved. Personal involvement in a conflict often breeds barbed humor that can be hurtful. As I arrived at a small conference where I was presenting, I heard participants joking about the food and the exercising, and telling "bathroom" jokes. The next day when I was teaching them to juggle with marshmallows, they began to throw the "juggling equipment" at each other as hard as they could and when the marshmallows fell to the floor, several people ground them into the carpet. Many of the group members looked angry and after we had lunch I realized what was happening. The organizers had taken a group of educators to a resort the day after school was out for the summer for a Wellness Conference. During the five days they were in attendance, they could not smoke or drink alcohol, were awakened at seven each morning to run or walk down the beach and were put on a salt-free, heavy-fiber diet. Apparently, the participants had nowhere to go to talk about their reactions to what was happening, a huge change in habits for some, so they used sarcasm and joked about it until they could get some of the emotion out.

Another way in which humor and laughter can helps us reach our goal of feeling like we belong is to eliminate barriers in communication and break the ice. Public speakers recognize the value of humor as an ice-breaker or a way to break through barriers by beginning a speech with a funny story. They realize this technique can help lower any reservations the audience might have either about the speaker or the topic. It makes people more approachable and provides a more comfortable avenue for interaction. Once our defenses, whatever they are, are breached, we start talking or listening, thereby promoting the possibility of more fruitful communication. Jim described a meeting he attended where two factions were allegedly trying to resolve a common issue. He said he sat there for about an hour and heard no progress being made, so he raised his hand and said, "I'm new but I notice we have been here for an hour and are no closer to a solution than when we started." The chair of the meeting acknowledged that Jim was new to this group, adding, "We have to go through the courting ritual first." Jim responded, "I don't know about you but I am ready to jump into the back seat." After a few seconds of shocked silence, then a hearty laugh, he noted some progress in the proceedings. His humor confronted the lengthiness of the ritual and lack of movement and served to move the group along to productivity. His humor made the obvious, obvious.

Many sensitive points can be softened using humor and, in some cases, it seems that the infusion of wit has the ability to help us more clearly understand or face painful or upsetting messages. Frequently, a funny message can get through our defenses and allow us to hear and see. In the past few years, newspaper cartoons on Thanksgiving Day depict hunger themes and help us realize others are not as fortunate as we are and open doors to discussing issues that are difficult to confront. One such cartoon was a picture of a starving child with a bite taken out of the picture. While the reality behind the image was certainly not funny, at the same time, it was difficult to ignore the fact that children were going hungry. The humor was subtle but the contrast between children dying of starvation and the typical gluttony at Thanksgiving time was profound. During the 60s, folk singers sang songs about issues that essentially were not funny, for example, the Kingston Trio's "They're Rioting in Africa," and the Chad Mitchell Trio's "Your Friendly Neighborhood Ku Klux Klan" and "The John Birch Society" thrust social issues into our awareness through satire and humor. Whether we feel hopeless, uninvolved, responsible, or angry, many of the painful messages we hear today do not reach us. The satire of the songs can break down fear, ignorance, or complacency so the underlying message can come across more clearly. We can speculate that the laughter opens our eyes so we can see things more plainly and the awareness that takes place can have a substantial impact on our behavior.

Humor is also believed to promote intimacy, belonging, warmth, and friendliness in groups (Block, Browning & McGrath, 1983). It increases participation in the experience of building relationships among group members that is characterized by naturalness and creates positive contact with others (Haig, 1986). Shared laughter deepens relationships and creates cohesion in the group. As the life of the group progresses, it can increase the level of intimacy in the group. This occurs as group members learn more about each other and about what is appropriate when laughing at interactions within the group. Alexander (1986) believes the social benefits are closely tied to the physiological benefits because it is the social situations that evoke laughter, which in turn causes physiological changes.

Physical Benefits

Laughing makes us feel good. Of course it does! When we laugh, we generate positive energy and we feel good, not to mention the release we get from a genuine belly laugh. Although mirth increases heart rate, blood pressure, and muscle tightness, these are temporary, and our body quickly returns to relaxation, so we can say hilarity relaxes us (Wilson, 1999). In a delightful article, Chafe (1987) postulates that the "basic, evolutionary, adaptive function (of humor) is a disabling one" (p. 18). He believes that humor is a "safety valve" that basically saves us from ourselves, from our taking things seriously when we should not. He notes the physiological reactions to laughter as being physically disabling. For example, there is an interference in normal breathing patterns which he says is in itself enough to put someone "out of commission," and there is evidence that when we laugh, we exhale more than we inhale, which compounds the disabling effect of humor, especially in situations where a "stable torso" is required. He points out that during this interference it is virtually impossible to exercise ("do push-ups") or work ("type a paper"). To further emphasize his point, he notes that research has shown that laughter decreases muscle tension and he concludes that during laughter, nothing productive can be accomplished physically. Not only that, but laughter also "contributes to the disablement of others" (p. 21). Laughter is contagious and it is one thing that is okay to spread around! His penultimate words on the subject are that "in the humor state you can't act effectively, and you like it" (p. 21). If you do not believe this, try to pick up something heavy when you are laughing hard. Once, two of us were unsuccessfully trying to load a desktop copier into the backseat of my car. The problem was that I did not have the original carton and we had to use the packing insulation form which was the shape of the bottom of the copier. We just could not fit it right. When we both started giggling, I noticed the copier was getting closer to the ground as my helper and I struggled to hang onto the machine. We hurriedly placed the machine in the car without the insulation to buffer it from the driving vibrations. Our laughter had relaxed us to the degree that we almost dropped the copier! The ridiculous part of this story is that I think we would have continued to laugh even if we had dropped the machine.

Norman Cousins' book, *Anatomy of an Illness* (1979), describes his recovery from a life-threatening illness. He watched *Candid Camera* tapes, Marx Brothers films, and other comedy programs and found after 10 minutes of laughter, he would have at least two hours of pain-free sleep. He later speculated that laughter and positive emotions, specifically "love, hope, faith, will to live, festivity, purpose, and determination" (Cousins, 1989, p. 212) stimulated the body's production of endorphin, a natural pain killer. While the effects of laughter on his recovery cannot be measured, his story is credited with popularizing the notion that humor and joyfulness have power to heal. In the mid 80s, a colleague and I had the pleasure of meeting with Mr. Cousins and we gave him a "Dorph" doll. During that time he told us of an "experiment" he tried on himself. He measured several enzymes in his blood, then sat and thought for five minutes about what a wonderful world this would be if only the United States had a sane, rational foreign policy. He commented, "You can understand my joy and elation." At the end of five minutes, he took another blood sample and measured the identical enzymes. He said they had all risen at least fifty percent (N. Cousins, personal communication, April 1986).

Laughter is aerobic. William Fry Jr. identifies laughter as a physical exercise and provides the following description:

> It causes huffing and puffing, speeds up the heart rate, raises blood pressure, accelerates breathing, increases oxygen consumption, gives the muscles of the face and stomach a workout, and relaxes muscles not involved in laughing. (cited in Cousins, 1989, p. 132)

He adds that twenty seconds of laughter can "double the heart rate for three to five minutes" and that is "the equivalent of ten minutes of strenuous rowing" (p. 132). Some people call this internal jogging, but it does not burn calories. Test this out with this simple aerobic exercise, designed to help you loosen up, that you can do anywhere. Sit in a chair with your feet flat on the floor. Start by moving your forehead to loosen it up. You will notice other parts of your face are moving so in a systematic manner do the following: scrunch up your eyes a few times, wiggle your nose, twist your lips around. Then stop and start rocking back and forth in your chair. After doing that a few times, each time you lean back pick up one of your feet and when you lean forward, stomp it down. Do that with each foot several times. Then, as you lean back and bring up one foot, also raise that arm. When you lean forward and stomp your foot, slap your hand on your thigh. Practice that a few times. Now you are ready to reap the aerobic benefits. Do all of these actions together and put a sound to it. To increase the effectiveness of this exercise, for example, to get you to laugh harder, you might want to sit in front of a mirror! Or, stick a nickel on your forehead and see if anyone notices it or says anything. If that does not get you to chuckle, you can always play tiddly winks by scrunching up your forehead and catching the coin in your hand. Have you ever hung a teaspoon off your nose? The purpose of these activities is to help you lighten up, to foster that playfulness that seems to get lost when we feel stressed.

Perhaps a little known benefit of laughter and one that has not been researched extensively is that it curbs hunger! For me, this idea surfaced in a seminar in Germany where participants reported they were not hungry for either lunch or dinner after spending the day laughing. Recently, Katie Overman wrote a book about this phenomenon, indicating she lost 35 pounds by laughing (cited in Oldenburg, 2005). Patch Adams, founder of the Gesundheit! Institute, and whose vision was to build the first silly hospital in history, one where having fun was a byword, explains, "The clearest connection [of laughter to weight-loss] is that depression, boredom and loneliness are the gigantic reasons why people eat gigantic quantities of trash and fatness." This weight loss, he surmised, comes about because of the "life that leads to laughter and the readiness to laugh" (*Seattle Times*, May 1, 2005, p. K4). This sounds like he is talking about the *Humor Perspective*.

"Laughter Clubs" are a recent phenomenon initiated in India by Madan Kataria. He noticed his more good-humored patients seemed to recover more quickly and decided he wanted to reap the benefits from hearty laughter before his work day, so he invited a group of people to join him in a laughter club. Steve Wilson, an American psychologist, is credited with bringing this technique to the United States and subsequently this group experience has spread throughout the world. People are being trained to run these "laughter groups" and we have only to look up "Laughing Clubs" on the Internet to find such a group or a trainer nearby. The description of these groups says that people get together and laugh for 45 minutes, usually in the morning and then go about their day in a refreshed state of mind. They advocate laughing stress away any-where from five or ten minutes to one hour and reiterate that this type of activity makes us feel good, brings people together, and alleviates stress.

Psychological Benefits

Humor is distracting. When we laugh, for that brief time, we change our focus. If we were feeling tense, hostile, angry, or sad in a particular situation, when we laugh we focus on whatever we find funny and, temporarily at least, divert our attention from the source of our stress. Through this means, laughter diffuses negative emotions. A director of a mental hospital described his method of distracting himself from feeling angry with his staff during meetings. He visualized himself with a large water pistol and each time someone said or did something to which he responded with negative feelings, he would "shoot" and imagine them drenched. He reported this got him through many trying meetings. Along the same vein, novice speakers are sometimes advised to think of the audience sitting there naked or in their underwear. One morning I got dressed for work in a hurry and in the dark. As I walked into my office building, I noticed I was walking funny, looked down, and saw I was wearing two different shoes, one slightly higher than the other, one black and one blue. Chuckling, I went into a college faculty meeting that was particularly contentious and I managed to avoid getting caught up in the conflict. Every time I was tempted to take sides, I thought about how these people were totally unaware of the fashion statement I was making for university professors.

Humor can distance us from pain and threat, giving us a respite. The laughter does not take away the pain permanently, but it gives the person a brief and welcome interlude before facing the hurt or grief again. I received a revealing email from Donna that demonstrates both her sense of humor and how she uses it to distance herself from distress:

I owe three years' back taxes I didn't know about until this week. I own a meth rental house that is boarded up. My daughter-in-law is a drug addict and is in jail. My grandchildren are in foster care. My 45-year-old son is out of work, living with me, and has a trial date of September 11th. But, wait, there is good news! I have car insurance with Geico." (DW, personal communication, August 2006)

Gallows humor, the type of humor that jokes about traumatic events, serves a defensive purpose. It can protect those who use it from the horrors they encounter in their daily work. Health care providers and soldiers are among the groups that are noted for using this type of humor. Being exposed to death, danger, and gut-wrenching fear or repeatedly experiencing profound loss is excruciating. It is possible these people laugh to keep from crying. Paul McGhee (2005) published a letter from an anesthetist to a child of a patient who died during surgery:

You saw me laugh after your father died. I was splashing water on my face at a sink midway between the emergency room lobby and the far green room where his body lay. Someone told a feeble joke and I brayed laughter like a jackass, decorum forgotten until I met your glance . . . your eyes streaming with tears.

My laugh was inappropriate, and for that I apologize. But it was a necessity. I laughed, nominally, at a corny joke. It's no secret that hospital people seem to enjoy warped humor . . . we're often too morbid. . . .It's not pleasant. Neither is hospital work, at times . . .

While we may appear emotionless behind our various masks, please understand: Much of the stress that health care workers suffer comes about because we do care. We cared about your father . . .

That day you saw me laugh, I knew that another patient was waiting who needed my care and full attention in surgery. As I stood at that sink and washed sweat and vomitus from my face and arms, my laugh was no less cleansing for me than were your tears for you.

A nurse in a seminar told a story about a funeral home experience over 20 years ago. Back in those days, when someone died, the wake was held for four or five days and the family was faced with the constancy of the grief elicited by the viewing. After this nurse's uncle died, each evening during the week the family came to sit with the body and greet the mourners. Each night they were directed to a different room in the mortuary. By the third night, one of the aunts found this upsetting and kept asking, "Why do they keep moving the body?" The response she got was, "They only move the heads."

Humor is not only useful in expressing ideas, feelings, or attitudes—it also allows us to be playful. Wearing a clown nose on the way home from work has been used effectively by some people to signal work is over. This might even cause another driver to smile. Kent used a red nose to help an employee relax:

I had a new hire who I asked to meet with me. I needed to describe a new assignment plus I was curious as to how things were going on the job. From others on the staff I learned that the young lady was terrified of "the boss." She
had anxiously questioned them as to why the boss wanted to talk to her. At the
appointed time she arrived visibly nervous. After she was seated, I announced
that before I could talk I would have to get into my management outfit. I turned
my back and put on a red clown nose. Swiveling back to face her, I proceeded
to conduct the meeting with no mention of the nose. After a shocked look and a
smile, the young woman became more relaxed as the meeting continued. The-
reafter, a meeting with "the boss" was no longer a negative issue for her. (K.
Olson, personal communication, June 2006)

Besides creating energy and lessening tension, laughter provides a means
for us to look at situations differently. One reason might be that when we laugh,
we become distracted from whatever the negative focus had been prior to that
response and a good laugh may stimulate more alternatives and an openness to
exploring new ideas. Part of this may be our recognition of the incongruities in
situations which, when these are funny, provide new insights (Martin, as cited in
Dingfelder, 2006). On the other hand, we can use humor to change someone
else's perspective, as Charlie, an events manager for the American Lung Association's cross country and West Coast Seattle to San Francisco fundraiser bike
rides, was trying to do:

Larry is a wonderful guy who comes from the great heartland (read: rural Indi-
ana) and clearly isn't used to life in the coastal regions (of either coast). He
came west a couple of years ago to volunteer on one of our bike rides. We had
a rest day in Fort Bragg, CA, and some friends and I rode into town from our
camp site looking forward to a real sit-down, "eat-it-in-a-restaurant" breakfast.
The first restaurant we came to looked nice (something perhaps more interesting than a Denny's). And I noticed Larry in the parking lot talking with one of
the other riders.

My friends walked inside and I walked over to see what they knew about the
place. I talked with Larry and the other rider for a moment, then started to walk
toward the restaurant with the other rider. Larry called me back and putting his
hand on my shoulder, he drew me close, waiting for the other rider to walk
away. He looked surreptitiously up and down the street (making sure no one
else was in earshot). Then he nodded toward the restaurant and said, "Charlie.
It's organic." I wasn't quite sure what he meant, then it dawned on me. I said
"you mean the food." "Yeah," he said with a concerned look. So I put my hand
on his shoulder and looked surreptitiously up and down the street and said,
"Larry. It's California." (C. Vanderberg, personal communication, May 10,
2006)

Humor also can help us remember things and can be an effective learning
tool. Research suggests using mirth in classrooms helps students be more moti-
vated and involved and dissipates anxiety. L. Berk (2002, cited in Stambor,

2006) and Wanzer (1999) (cited in Stambor, 2006) both indicated the type of humor used in classrooms must be pertinent to the subject. In addition, Wanzer's research revealed that teachers using wit were viewed as "more competent communicators and more responsive to students' needs than dry instruction" (Wanzer, 1999, p. 61). The author warned about its overuse and relevance to the topic to be learned. Stress is placed on the benefits to the students not the instructor. R. Berk (cited in Stambor, 2006) stated, "What I do and how I teach is all about the students. It has nothing to do with me. I'm tapping into *their* multiple intelligence needs and *their* culture so that *they* can understand the material in *their* terms" (p. 64). Later, he observes that the use of humor at time of student anxiety (e. g., prior to testing) can ease tension and positively impact performance (in Stambor, 2006). Some of his suggestions for infusing humor into classes are:

- Make your syllabus funny: insert funny comments, ridiculous office hours, strange prerequisites, etc.
- Bring in relevant cartoons or articles from the newspaper. One article published last January (2005), which could have been useful then, was titled "It's almost official: Today's the 'worst' day of the year." The article explains January 24th is the day that all "the rotten things we humans must face in life peak in late January." He identifies the "rotten things" as being: the date is too far from Christmas to look forward to that holiday and too recent to "have recovered from it financially," winter weather is bad compared to other times of year, by the 24th we will have dumped our New Year's resolutions and are smoking, drinking and overeating, shortterm there are no three-day weekends and our tax forms are in the mail. (The Seattle Times, January 24, p. 2.)
- In a question and answer period, interject questions like "How many of you don't care?" or "How many of you don't like to be awakened during class?"
- Exaggerate questions, examples, etc. (in Stambor, 2006, p. 64)

One way we learn about what is in the market place is from television advertisements. If we attend to them, more frequently than not, most of us tend to remember those that are funny. Think about television commercials. Which ones do you remember, if any? Were they funny or deadly serious? We have a greater tendency to remember what tickled us or, as a friend noted, those that irritate us the most. I remember one where a car salesman was standing next to a car with his mother. He expounded on all of the things this car could do. His claims became more and more outrageous. Then he stopped and said, "May lightning strike my mother is this isn't true." Immediately there was a lightening bolt. While I did not go out and buy the car, I still remember the look on the salesman's face.

When we consciously look for positives in situations we consider negative, there is almost always something funny. Going through an Internal Revenue Service audit is not considered a humorous experience, and you can imagine my anxiety as we walked through my return and as I tried to respond to the questions about things that had occurred a few years ago. The auditor was very nice and was trying to educate me as to what she was doing. Even though I appreciated her attitude and she assured me I was bright enough to do my own taxes, my tension did not abate. All of a sudden, I noticed the sign on her wall, "I can only please one person per day. Today is not your day. Tomorrow doesn't look good either." I laughed and some of my tension evaporated. Then I was better able to appreciate her courtesy and concern as she attempted to "retrain" me.

There remains much to be learned about humor, laughter and positive attitudes and the resulting impact on us both psychologically and physically. There is evidence these responses are helpful in social, psychological and physical ways, but can they "cure"? No one has proved this conclusively. Reviewers of research about the impact of humor or laughter indicate that laughter and positive attitudes and feelings *may* impact physical and mental health; however, there are other positive emotions and behaviors that have been offered as reasonable explanations for changes in health (Martin, 2001; Mahony, 2000). Berk and Tan's (1999) research has demonstrated laughter does impact us physiologically; Berk, Tan, and Westengard (2006) noted, "It may sound corny but we in the health care medical sciences need to 'get serious about happiness' and the lifestyle that produces it, relative to mind, body and spirit and its biotranslation" (p. 58). McGhee (1999) noted research is limited but does agree laughter has the ability to protect one against immunosuppression during stressful times. So while current opinions vary as to whether laughter and humor impact physical health, those of us who present humor seminars and workshops certainly believe it!

Chapter 3

Obstacles to Using Humor

If humor and laughter are so good for us, why not use them more often? Why do we shy away from using humor? Some of us have not thought about why. Still, others of us refrain from laughing because of a fear which may not be rational. Below are a few reasons seminar participants have said they are cautious about using humor.

"I Am Not Funny"

When people are convinced that they are not funny, they will not attempt to be humorous. It does not matter whether this message came from bad experiences or from being told by others, the result is the same. "I do not have a sense of humor" is a phrase I hear occasionally in the workshops. While that could be true, there may be another, more accurate reason. We get messages about humor from early interactions in our environment, and although these messages may be subtle, we learn. If we have been in an environment where humor is not utilized (effectively) or one where humor is used in destructive ways, we might not develop a sense of what is funny and what is not, or even what is appropriate and what is not. However, in many cases, it is our lack of the confidence that prevents us from risking the use of humor in a situation. There has to be a sensitivity to those who are involved and to the situation before humor is interjected.

Part of this awareness comes from listening closely both to what people say and what they do not say, verbal and nonverbal cues. These indicators are found through observation of the types of humor that appear to be appreciated, how the person(s) responds to others' joking, and the relationship between the humorist and the subject of the humor. By doing this, we can understand more about the subject's sense of humor and can use our wit more effectively. Klein (1989) provided this example of the necessity of listening for indications about what another person thinks is funny:

> At an international meeting of top-ranking company officials, one executive from America asked another executive from Japan what the Japanese regarded as the most important language for world trade. The American expected the answer would be English, but the executive from Japan smiled and replied, "My customer's language." (Klein, 1989, p. 35)

Listen to the other person's language and topics of discussion. Which topics make the person laugh? Does the person laugh about a personal characteristic or habit? If so, that is probably a safe subject for us to laugh about as well. For example, someone who jokes about alphabetizing the canned food in the pantry will be more likely to laugh when we joke about it than if we knew this was a characteristic of the person but had never heard him or her laugh about it. Listen and learn.

"Laughing is Not Professional"

For many people, the image of a "professional" precludes demonstrating a sense of humor. For them, being professional is serious business. Several years ago, a "Creative Humor at Work" seminar was rejected by the American Counseling Association with the notation, "Not appropriate to ACA audiences." Apparently one of the reviewers thought counseling was too serious to bring humor into the mix. In another instance, a search committee member at a university noted after a humor presentation, "Humor is not academic." The image of such a professional is usually modeled on someone else, perhaps a role model, who is never seen laughing. Being a professional is serious; however, when applied sensitively, the use of humor can be effective here, too.

When I work with a client doing a learning style assessment, I look for opportunities to say something funny and point out or respond to something funny to help a client laugh and relax. One way I do this is to laugh when the client says something funny, as long as the client is also laughing. My goal is always to help clients relax and give their best performance in order to gather accurate data. One example occurred when a client was asked a question about the speed of light, the client responded, "Really, really fast." We both laughed. Instead of feeling defensive about not knowing the answer, she visibly relaxed and appeared more at ease with the ensuing testing. As we progress through an assessment, I am aware of clues to my clients' sense of humor, for instance, do they smile or laugh and at what or when do they make humorous comments. Based on my perceptions, I may interject comments that I judge to be appropriate to what I see and hear. After the client has responded to a question, and if the time is right, I might relate a humorous response someone else made to that item. It must work because many clients comment that the assessment was fun!

A corollary of laughter being seen as unprofessional is the belief or perception that people in a particular occupation or field are not supposed to be funny. Based on our own experiences, we may think that corporate officers, school board members, clergy, and so on (substitute your image) are not "funny." People in responsible positions may be seen as competent only when they are serious, so they stay serious to be seen as competent. An example of such a situation happened during a Christmas Eve program at church when a child recited his Christmas "piece" and did not quite "get it right." The congregation laughed. The minister rose and said, "We do not laugh in the house of the Lord."

This is certainly not true of all contemporary clergy. My friend Tom, a Presbyterian minister, asked a professional clown to come into the Easter service. The clown used a huge earth ball to play catch with the congregation. The joy and laughter was wonderful to experience. When asked about his reasoning, Tom indicated Christians experience both sadness and joy during this church holiday. Clowns with their sad or happy faces have a marvelous way of helping people feel and deal with these two emotions. He thought the clown reminded the congregation in church that it is okay to have feelings about Jesus. Tom said:

> At the beginning of worship the clown and I strategized that we needed something surprising and enjoyable to get the Easter celebration started . . . something that spoke powerfully to the joy of resurrection and would wake people up to this wonderful moment in the world's history. We thought it would be awesome to bring in a huge ball filled with air and have the congregation, much like many "gathered people" in North America, play with one of those huge balls like we were at some mega event. The clown really wanted an activity that allowed young and old to participate and drew people together as a family. The children's message became a critical piece to the clown's story telling for the morning, because we figured many would not really understand why a huge ball of air represented the celebration of the resurrection for us, and so our clown followed up by retelling the story of Jesus' death and resurrection. He used an inflated balloon, enjoyed playing with and then ultimately popped it. Miming being sad, he buried it in the trunk, and then heard pounding coming from the trunk. Our Clown's sadness became joy when he opened the trunk and out "floated" a new kind of balloon, not one that was filled with stale air, but one that was filled with hot air and could fly around. We thought that this would connect with the kids and the rest of the church—the fact that this new balloon was shaped in a heart was that we were hopeful it reminded people of God's love and that God loved Jesus so much God resurrected Jesus to be with God forever. My hope was that by the end of the morning everyone would have understood that God wants us to live with him forever as well, and Easter is a wonderful celebration of God's love for us. (T, Lobaugh, personal communication, September, 11, 2006

Tom reported that while his creativity was not accepted by everyone, many responded favorably.

Another time, I had done a "Creative Humor at Work" seminar for some of the congregation, and the next day Tom, dressed in his clerical garb, welcomed

"The Humor Lady" (me!) to the church service while wearing a clown nose. So, beware of people who believe they have to appear serious in order for others to think them competent. You might get hoodwinked into not having fun with your work!

"They're Not Going to Laugh"

It is true that others might not laugh when we say something we think is funny. Would that be the end of the world? Will you die immediately? Yes, it might be momentarily embarrassing, but if this is the source of the fear, it can be overcome. What is so awful about being embarrassed and what can you learn from this experience? If this is a consistent response to your attempts at humor, and you still think what you said was funny, you might take a look at what went wrong and ask yourself some of these questions:

- Was the comment genuinely funny?
- Was it appropriate to the situation or group?
- Was the timing right?
- What was your purpose in saying something funny at that particular time? Were you trying to lighten up or divert a discussion, bring attention to your wit or prove you belong?

There will be times when you might be the only one who thinks your comment is funny, and in this case, you might consider keeping the comment to yourself. If your joking falls flat again and again, and if after self-searching you really believe you were funny and that your remark conformed to the acceptable type of humor for this group, you have other choices. You might want to consider whether these are the type of people with whom you want to associate, or if you do continue be part of this group, keep your humor to yourself and enjoy your own comedy. Remember, humor does not always have to be shared for you to enjoy it.

"People Will Laugh at Me, Not with Me"

One of the biggest threats many of us carry from childhood is, "If you do that, someone will laugh at you." This fear is a powerful manipulator of our behavior since it frequently restricts our risk-taking behavior. What will happen if someone does laugh? If we take time to ask ourselves that question, we will most likely answer, "Not much!" Comedians often have a tag line when they say something funny and the audience does not laugh. They might say something like, "Is anybody out there?" "Is anyone home?" or even "Did you get that?" This usually draws a response of some type and the better performers play off of the response.

"Others Will Not See Me as Serious"

When we become adults, it becomes important to be seen as an adult with a commitment to making a contribution. The fear seems to be that if I am not seen as a serious adult, I am not respected and if I am not respected no one will listen to what I say or have confidence or trust in my judgment. You might verify this by asking others to see if your observation about the necessity of appearing serious all the time is correct, or watch others to see if anyone is serious all of the time. If they do laugh, when? Be sensitive to the situation and the people in it. Sometimes we assume that we must be serious in order to be respected when, if we carefully observe others, laughter is not only acceptable, but enhances respect. Timing is always a consideration. Using humor at an inappropriate time can be detrimental. It may interfere with the process or progress of the interaction, hurt someone's feelings, or be seen as a sign of disrespect.

"I Would Look Foolish"

Hugh Prather (1970) commented that if he was not afraid to "just be me," he would be naturally funny. He refers to an internal censor that we all seem to have to some degree. Klein (1989) noted the Fool was admired in medieval times for his ability make people laugh and Klein believes being seen as foolish or doing "foolish" things can brighten up gloom and doom. When was the last time you did something foolish and how was it perceived? A colleague and I went to meet another colleague, Jim, at the airport. One of us dressed as a clown complete with face makeup and wig, and the other wore an eagle face mask. We sat in seats across from and facing the exit gate. As passengers emerged, many of them did a doubletake and smiled or laughed. As Jim exited, he laughed and said, "I think I know these two clowns." On the way back to the car, it seemed like all of the children in the terminal came up to see us. The children looked delighted and their parents were all smiling. Our initial reticence turned to a discussion of when we could do this again.

Culture dictates acceptability and rules for the use of humor. In many cultures women are not supposed to be funny. Look at pictures of women during the Victorian age. You will seldom, if ever, see a woman smile. There could be many reasons for this. One speculation has been that laughing would cause wrinkles. Another is that laughing is not feminine, or perhaps life was just difficult, or maybe they had bad dentists, or any number of other possibilities. Some psychologists have labeled the use of humor as "an aggressive act" (Freud, 1966) and have believed women should not be seen as aggressive, the cultural antithesis of being feminine. Describing the American culture, Barreca (1991) noted "Good Girls didn't crack jokes, Bad Girls did. A Good Girl's sense of humor was laughing at boys' jokes, especially when the jokes were at the girl's expense." (p. 1). So, it was fine for girls to laugh at boys' jokes about them but not to make jokes themselves or about themselves. McGhee (1999) concurs by noting that after age six, girls who cling to society's "rules of femininity" tend to smile rather than laugh aloud at jokes and, in turn, and because of these rules, tend to tell fewer and safer jokes, those that adhere to the "rules." Also, many of these women laugh at men's humor as a way to support them.

While these rules have changed to some degree, there is still evidence of restrictions on women and their humor. Those that rebel often subscribe to a feminist approach to comedy that directly confronts social norms. Lucille Ball, Gracie Allen, Goldie Hawn, Lily Tomlin, Gilda Radner, Mary Tyler Moore, and Carol Burnett are examples of exceptions of women who broke through barriers to women's being funny. They were successful using their own unique styles of slapstick humor, which in many cases was self-deprecating. Other successful humorists such as Erma Bombeck, Jean Kerr, Phyllis Diller, and Joan Rivers also used a self-effacing style. In more recent years, many women who have attempted to "break into" the comedy field have sounded very much like their male counterparts and many have not been successful. Those who have succeeded have found their own style. Barrett (n.d.) noted there are two types of female humor: feminist humor that makes fun of a society that needs to change and female humor that perpetuates existing norms.

We do not all laugh at the same things and each of us considers certain things just not funny. In our world today, culture also dictates which topics are fair to make fun of and which are not. Humor that attacks values is generally not considered funny by those who adhere to those values. It may be permissible to laugh at some topics if you are a member of that culture. However, if you are not, it is wiser to accept that as an outsider it would be considered inappropriate and disrespectful for you to make jokes about something considered sacred by that cultural group. In past months, there have been instances where the Quran was the topic of cartoons and the Muslim public outrage was colossal, prolonged, and violent. It is crucial for us to be sensitive to and acknowledge cultural diversity and cultural values systems and refrain from making fun of those whose beliefs differ from ours. For many people and in many cultures, to ridicule another person's values is unacceptable.

Consider a recent natural disaster in America, hurricane Katrina. Many people find it difficult, if not impossible, to find humor in such a tragedy. An article in the Washington Post ("New Orleans Hurricane Humor"; reprinted in The Seattle Times, February 28, 2006) describes the tentative uses of humor about the New Orleans catastrophe and the writer observes, "If humor is the best medicine, storm-shocked New Orleans is still tinkering with the dosage" (p. 14). The writer further identified some themes for floats in the parades celebrating Mardi Gras: "C'est Levee," "Girls Gone Wild," and "Corpse of Engineers." The writer also questioned whether it is funny or appropriate to ridicule such a disaster. What do you think? What are the parameters of humor when the topic is serious or sensitive?

An interesting phenomenon occurs when we do risk expressing our humor. If people laugh, it bolsters our ego and makes it easier to hazard saying something funny the next time. With a few successes under our belt, people begin to know us and expect us to be funny; they expect to laugh and generally do. In a sense, you could say we train others to laugh at our wit.

As each of us contemplates personal issues that get in the way of being funny, we must consider if our wit is helpful or hurtful. The power of humor evident in satire, sarcasm and irony expresses differences that can separate people or can bring them together. Cartoonists, satirists and stand-up comedians can get away with using insulting or cutting humor to express feelings and thoughts about issues or people for us, ones we may be unwilling or unlikely to express ourselves. By voicing our own thoughts and feelings or voicing what we may be thinking and not saying, they let us "off the hook" and allow us to sit back and enjoy with no risk to us. The threat for us may be fear of offending or being rejected by our peers, or we may have deeply-felt emotions underlying our values, which makes us unable to see anything funny about specific behaviors. Still, we may laugh heartily (or uncomfortably) at a comedian's description. An unspoken rule in this situation is, you speak for me.

Humor can be employed both as a constructive tool and as a destructive tool. Constructive humor brings about positive effects while destructive humor is used to hurt. Joel Goodman, Director of the Humor Project (Baum, 1998), once said, "Destructive humor goes for the jugular vein while constructive humor goes for 'the jocular vein'" (p. 3). Sometimes the person using humor is not trying to hurt intentionally, but is simply demonstrating a lack of sensitivity to another's circumstance or values.

Positive humor builds self esteem; negative humor erodes self esteem. Think about situations when children use humor. When the target person laughs, the child smiles in return and will likely try for another smile. We feel good about ourselves when we receive a positive response, and this helps teach us what types of humor are appropriate and in which situations it is appropriate to use humor. We learn to search for cues for when to use humor and we learn from role models. When my nephew, Gavin was 12, he told me he wanted to develop his sense of humor. He confided he wanted to model his father except sometimes his father's humor was "really sick" and sometimes "really funny" so he said he was aiming for the middle road. Currently he is still experimenting. Sometimes he is "really funny" and sometimes, when we do not laugh, he learns he is really not, but he is learning about cues and timing and becoming more conscious of differences. He is learning to be alert to and to gauge reactions he receives in order to understand others' senses of humor better. We were playing cards during a recent visit and he noisily slapped his hand on the table as he discarded. I commented, "You did that just like your dad." He responded, "The nut doesn't fall far from the tree."

Adolescents learn about humor from role models and they also learn from each other. This is illustrated by Elena, a music teacher, who tells this story which describes another adolescent who was learning to be sensitive to women. While it was not meant to be funny, it was:

One of my favorite stories from teaching (music) is of an adolescent who had been my student for years, since he was seven years old, so we knew each other well. One day I had a headache and hadn't slept well the night before and was in a kind of funk and the (piano) lesson wasn't going very well. Finally after about 10 minutes, he asked me if I was mad at him. I said, "No, it's not you. I'm just having a hard time; I don't feel all that great." He looked at me seriously and asked, "Is it that time of month?" I couldn't stop myself from smiling. "No," I said, "but thanks for asking." He then told me that he and his friends had been sitting around talking about things they understood they were NOT to say to girls. He thought he'd try one out on me. (E. Richmond, Personal Communication, May 11, 2006)

It is not a far stretch to surmise teenagers learn about what is funny in this way too, through gathering information and then testing it out.

Positive humor stimulates energy and creates open environments where new thoughts or ideas can flourish. Conversely, negative or hostile humor can create an atmosphere where people are unwilling to volunteer ideas for fear that they will be ridiculed or sanctioned in some way. Think about discussions in which you have been a part. Was humor used? Did people laugh? If so, what happened next?

As a member of the OK Chorale, I was once invited to play my autoharp. This was a risk as I had not played this instrument for long and never with a group. We were practicing a new song, one that I had not played before. The whole thing sounded terrible and we all knew it. When we finished the director looked at me and asked, "What do you think happened?" My response, "I was playing the wrong notes." A second of silence and everyone started laughing, and we started again, with renewed energy, and there were smiles when we finished.

Laughing "with" someone is supportive and creates cooperation while laughing "at" someone, as opposed to laughing "at" a situation to overcome it, is belittling and creates resistance and hostility. Since laughter is attractive and breaks down barriers, it is more useful to use humor to create a positive atmosphere where people and new ideas are valued. If people are feeling defensive as a result of being laughed at, it will be difficult to elicit creative or productive interchanges. No one wants to be put down or judged in negative ways. An example of this: I was given a one-hour PowerPoint presentation to present to a group, a program that I had not created and a topic with which I had little experience. Also, I had never used PowerPoint before. I spent many hours learning and preparing my presentation. The morning of the presentation, I got up early to go over the program one more time, then traveled out to the site. I followed my directions and got lost, made several U-turns but finally arrived at my destination. The person for whom I was waiting was tied up and it was 45 minutes later when she came into the waiting area to see me. After I introduced myself, she said, "Oh, your presentation isn't until tomorrow." I checked my calendar and she was right. Now, she could have laughed at me for being a day early, (or being a nitwit); however, I beat her to it since the presentation was on time management. Then we both enjoyed the irony. So did the participants the next day when I told the story and did the program! It would have been hard to go back and do the program the next day if she and the receptionist had laughed at me instead of with me.

An atmosphere characterized by positive humor creates a stimulating and creative environment distinguished by cooperation and acceptance and conveys sensitivity to others. In such an environment, people can thrive and grow. Negative humor creates distance, barriers, and an unwillingness to risk disclosing new ideas or thoughts. Think about a group to which you have belonged, either social or professional. How free were you to express your thoughts or feelings? When you felt uncomfortable about the possible reaction of others in the group and/or being the focus of joking, how willing were you to risk speaking? If you thought you were a respected member of the group, of equal status, you might have enjoyed the teasing as part of belonging to the group. Teasing can build cohesion or can create a "status hierarchy" (Prelle, 2006, p. 8) If you did not think you had the group's respect, there would have been a connotation of meanness and disrespect in the teasing (Encyclopedia of 20th Century American Humor, cited in McCahn, n.d., Putdowns and Rejoinders section). When you first joined this group, how willing were you to joke or make humorous comments? Often, people wait a period of time before expressing these comments. How long did it take you? When I first joined the OK Chorale, although many people were joking throughout the practices, it was not until I had sung with the group for more than a term and felt like I was accepted, did I verbally contribute to the camaraderie.

Destructive humor tends to focus on negatives in situations or people and says more about the deliverer than the focus person. Laughing at someone is frequently used indirectly as a means to express anger or displeasure. It can also be a means to deflect attention from the deliverer or unacceptable attributes of the deliverer. The target of the humor is not always the culprit. Also, joking at someone else's expense is meant to elevate the deliverer. Using humor in a constructive way helps focus on positive aspects and can help someone reframe a situation or experience and allow creative solutions to problems. Klein (1989) observed, "Whether you are using humor to ease your own dilemma or someone else's, the best rule to use is the AT&T principle: Make sure it is Appropriate, Timely, and Tasteful" (p. 36). He cautions against using jokes as a primary resource of humor and noted, "most of us cannot tell a joke well, and . . . jokes are often offensive" (p. 37). He seems to be emphasizing the use of a broader humor attitude, the *Humor Perspective*.

Chapter 4

Gender Differences

Men and women typically prefer different types of humor. John, a psychologist friend, told about his son's early hunting experience:

> When my son was 10 years old he had a slingshot that he loved to use for shooting at anything that moved—or not. His dream was to shoot one of the small red squirrels that frequented our bird feeder. One winter day he spotted a squirrel in a tree near the feeder. He frantically put on winter gear and pocketed several of the slingshot rocks he had gathered over the summer. With slingshot in hand he quietly crept up on the tree where the squirrel sat about 10 feet above the ground. As my son approached the tree, the squirrel moved to put the tree between himself and my son, leaving only part of his head exposed to danger from the slingshot. My son, attempting to get a clear shot, moved slowly around the tree. The squirrel, in an effort to stay hidden always stayed on the opposite side of the tree from my son. Suddenly my son carefully laid his slingshot on the ground, picked up a nearby stick and began to beat on the tree. The squirrel predictably raced up the tree and was gone. My son stood there gazing up into the tree, and then dejectedly picked up his slingshot and return to the house. My friend and I were dumbstruck at my son's behavior then burst into laughter. As my son entered the house I asked him what in the world he expected to happen when he beat on the tree with a stick. His response was "I was trying to scare the squirrel down the trees so I could get a good shot at him." (J. DeRuyter, personal communication, May 30, 2006).

As he told the story, John was laughing, but I was not. Once he explained that when a tree is shaken, the squirrel's instinct is *not* to come down, I understood. I had been focusing on the squirrel and hunting. He observed that every time he tells that story to others, men laugh but women do not. He added:

When I tell this story to couples (in therapy) the men invariably laugh and un-derstand its meaning. They understand the relationship between the beating the tree and creating an unsafe environment for their wives. On the other hand, women often have a very difficult time understanding the message and don't see the story as funny. They seem to focus on the fact that the intent of my son striking the tree was ultimately to harm the squirrel rather than to induce a spe-cific desired behavior. This relates to the gender-based notion of women being nurturers. As I wrote [this], I found myself really thinking about why men and women respond so differently to [the story]. I really do think that experience of relationship is an important part. I also have observed that generally men are far more "visual" than women and tend to "get" metaphors and stories more easily. Another possible influence is that when I use the story, the couples are general-ly experiencing significant conflict. When individuals are in conflict, to agree with the other (even about what is funny or helpful) can feel like giving in.

He continued:

I make some significant intuitive jumps with this, but the parallel that seems to be understood is that you can't scare a squirrel down a tree equals you can't demand a relationship with someone. If you want the squirrel to come down the tree (and closer to you) it has to feel safe—if it does not feel safe it runs away. If you want a person to increase intimacy (emotional or otherwise) with you, you must make the relationship feel safe—if the relationship does not feel safe, intimacy decreases. I truly don't understand why most guys seem to understand this almost intuitively. Women get it with a brief explanation, but there is sel-dom an "aha" moment involved. My suspicion has been, though not confirmed, is that they are being a bit resistant. (How's that for an explanation that leaves me blameless???) I actually don't think knowledge of hunting has anything to do with it. Anytime a relationship becomes competitive rather than cooperative I move towards this story. Actually the less tension that exists in the relation-ship the better this story works. The defenses are so high in truly abusive rela-tionships that nobody tends to get it. (J. DeRuyter, personal communication, May 30, 2006.

While we would like to believe society has changed significantly, there are still gender stereotypes as DeRuyter noted in the example above. McGhee (1979) noted there is little difference between the amount of laughing boys and girls do until the age of six. At that time, girls begin to respond to humor in more passive ways, especially those who are being taught the "rules" of being feminine. Eagly and Steffen (1986) tie these stereotypes to existing social roles and the unequal power structure between men and women (in Prelle, 2006). So-cially, males and females are assigned roles along with the expected behaviors that go with these roles. When one of us acts in a non-prescribed manner, there may be sanctions. In order to be seen in the most positive light by those deemed important to the us, we conform to what is expected, often a stereotypic beha-vior. Because of these stereotypes, we learn to expect certain gender-specific behaviors from each other, and learning how to use and to respond to humor differently is one such behavior. Prelle (2006) identified some of these differences as:

> Women are expected to fulfill the roles of supporter, be less aggressive and assertive, and display features of femininity that reflect a caring, soothing, and yielding nature. Men . . . are expected to assert themselves and be more aggressive. Because humor can be considered an aggressive act (Freud, 1966), it is reasonable to hypothesize that men are the joke-tellers and women are the joke-appreciators because of those traits, stereotypes, and roles that are prescribed to each gender. Men, who believe themselves to be of higher status than females, have the "right" to joke, while women are expected to be more passive and restrained. Thus, a woman who commands the attention of the group to tell a joke (or worse, a lewd joke) creates a disjunction between the stereotypes and roles associated with femininity and the aggressive nature of telling a joke. (Prelle 2006, p. 12)

Years ago I heard a joke and related it to my brother. On a visit to our parents' home, he repeated it with some embellishments. Our mother laughed but noted it was slightly off color. My brother said, "Don't blame me, I heard it from Sis." She looked at me and said, "Sandra" in a "that is not appropriate" voice. While her laughter had seemed somewhat uncomfortable when Sandy told the joke, she would not have responded with laughter had I told it.

Prelle's (2006) review of the research documented specific differences between men and women in their appreciation of humor. She noted, "Women are generally less inclined to tell jokes in mixed-sex company, although they do so when with other women" (p. 12). She speculated this may be the "result of socialization and the stereotypes associated with femininity that considers the use of aggressive humor inappropriate." (p. 12) Thus, anyone acting outside of the norm, whether male or female, creates a dissonance in the listeners.

The results of Prelle's (2006) study support the idea that it is more acceptable for men to tell jokes with sexual connotations than for women to do so, and she concluded this is because of our socialized rules of appropriate gender behavior. Basically, men are expected to use masculine forms of expression and women feminine-type responses. If this is true, a primary difference between men and women in their preferences of humor will reflect their learned beliefs about what is gender-appropriate, and these beliefs are generated by their societal experiences.

Let's go back to the squirrel hunting story. It makes sense to me that I did not laugh at the young boy's experience since I am not a hunter and have not had the experience of hunting prey in the woods. Once the reason for the laughter was explained, I could relate it to a female term used fairly recently for meeting men—"hustling," which is similar to hunting prey. If the story talked about "hustling," I would have caught on! About using this story in therapy, John indicated:

I have used this story many times. Sometimes it's with a demanding nagging wife, other times it's with a controlling or abusive husband, but one or the other attempts to compel the other to "love" them and to meet their emotional needs. Their goal is to get emotional needs met, but they don't understand that those needs can only be met in the context of relationship. They substitute behavioral demands for relationship and the effect of those demands is of course to "scare the squirrel up the tree." Much could be speculated about why men and women react so differently to this story. Often, with some explanation women will admit they get the point, but are usually unhappy and grudging about it. I think the difference is more about how men and women think about relationships. Men tend to be fairly simplistic (if I want the squirrel down the tree I need a handful of sunflower seeds) and women focus more on the nuances (but you intended to harm the squirrel). Men identify more with the hunter and women more with the squirrel? I'm not sure. (J. DeRuyter, personal communication, May 30, 2006)

I am consistently struck by gender differences in responding to humor at baseball games. When the video on "Baseball Bloopers" is shown, it seems to me, men laugh more than women at segments that show players crashing into walls or each other, while women laugh more at those players who overrun the ball, miss a catch or trip while running to a base, and then proceed to crawl the rest of the way. Women tend to express concern rather than laugh about those who run into walls or flip over fences. Men seem to laugh uncomfortably, perhaps identifying with the pain. Rather than making a judgment about these responses, it makes more sense to realize that men and women notice different aspects of an event.

While it is true that there are differences between styles and responses to jokes and wit, many women are learning about ways to be more active in creating humor, by taking risks to be funny. Evidence of women's rebellion to this stereotyping is found in the following jokes that were forwarded to me (I. Dode, personal communication, June 22, 2006):

Real Women Do Things A Little Differently

Ladies—If you accidentally over-salt a dish while it's still cooking, drop in a peeled potato and it will absorb the excess salt for an instant fix-me-up.
Real Woman—If you over-salt a dish while you are cooking, that's just too bad. Please recite with me, The Real Women's motto: I made it and you will eat it and I don't care how bad it tastes.

Ladies—Cure for headaches: Take a lime, cut it in half, and rub it on your forehead. The throbbing will go away.
Real Woman—Take a lime, mix it with tequila, chill, and drink. You might still have the headache, but who cares?"

Ladies—Stuff a miniature marshmallow in the bottom of a sugar cone to prevent ice cream drips.

Real Woman—Just suck the ice cream out of the bottom of the cone, for Pete's sake. You are probably lying on the couch, with your feet up, eating it anyway.

Ladies—To keep potatoes from budding, place an apple in the bag with the potatoes.
Real Woman—Buy boxed mashed potato mix and keep it in the pantry for up to a year.

Ladies—When a cake recipe calls for flouring the baking pan, use a bit of the dry cake mix instead and there won't be any white mess on the inside of the cake.
Real Woman—Go to the bakery—they'll even decorate it for you.

Ladies—If you have a problem opening jars, try using latex dishwashing gloves. They give a non-slip grip that makes opening jars easy.
Real Woman—Go ask the very cute neighbor guy to do it.

Ladies—Don't throw out all that leftover wine. Freeze into ice cubes for future use in casseroles and sauces.
Real Woman—Leftover wine??

Think of your own early experiences surrounding humor. As you think about your childhood experiences, what do you remember about types of humor that were used? Or, was humor used? Describe messages about humor you received from significant adults in your life prior to age 10. Were these subtle gender-related messages, for example, females always laugh at male's jokes or males are the ones expected to tell jokes? Did males tell jokes making fun of or belittling women? Who was the person(s) who gave you these messages? What makes you laugh now? Describe two things about which you have laughed during the past several days. As you respond to these questions, can you discover how any of these early messages impact your sense of humor today?

Chapter 5

Humor in Relationships—
How can I Infuse the *Humor Perspective* in My Relationships?

When asked if a good sense of humor is important in a relationship, most people will say "Yes, extremely important!" (Campbell, 2005). While there are differences between females and males in their expression of and response to humor, in conversations about characteristics preferred in one's life partner, a sense of humor and an appreciation of humor are usually at or near the top of the list. Prelle's (2006) investigation discovered men and women have different definitions of what constitutes a good sense of humor in the other sex. In differing order of importance, both genders described a partner with "the ability to laugh at one's self and/or situation" and "a sharp wit." Men added someone "who smiles a lot, laughs a lot" and has the ability to understand and/or relate to their [the man's] sense of humor", that is, appreciate their sense of humor. Women identified as additional preferences for men "the ability to be quick on one's feet, come up with 'comebacks' and original one-liners," that is, the ability to create humor, and "a sense of humor that shows they have self confidence" (p. 22). In Bressler and Balshine's (2006) study, women indicated a preference for a sense of humor in men. However, men did not identify wit as a preferential characteristic for women. They concluded this confirmed a stereotype of gender differences. Although there seem to be gender differences in responding to and creating humor, one thing we do know is that positive humor builds relationships and allows them to grow while negative humor creates tension and restricts healthy interactions. Each of us have seen or been in both types of relationships.

Snyder and Cabianca (1972) described all ongoing relationships as evolving through a series of eight stages: meeting, getting acquainted, caring, conflict, separation, reconciliation, deeper level of caring, and final parting. Recognizing that a relationship can leap from any one of these steps to a final parting, humor or mirth can be beneficial in each step.

When we first *meet* someone we make decisions as to whether we want any further contact. During this initial phase, often there is some level of tension, or in some cases, anxiety. Aron (cited in Stambor, 2006) noted that it is natural for people to want to associate with others but that this desire often causes anxiety. As noted earlier, humor breaks the ice and distracts from that fear. Further exploration is needed to learn about this other person. Humor can be utilized as a way to help both parties reduce tension and relax so the relationship can progress. Indirectly this is also a method used to see which topics are acceptable and which topics cause the other person to react with laughter. Simultaneously, humor keeps the atmosphere light. An ad campaign for the Mariners Baseball Club's Singles Night promotion listed some examples of ice breakers: "I lost my telephone number. Can I have yours?" or "You know that gizmo that opens car doors? I invented that." Heather, a lawyer, contributed the following:

> A very attractive young woman in a bar was the object of several males' attention. They approached her one by one but she did not respond positively to any of them. Ultimately a man came up to her and said, "I'm rich." She answered, "You're buying." Still another, a woman sitting at a table in a bar was confronted by a gentleman who said, "Every time I come in you are here." The woman responded, "This is the first time I have been here." He said, "Me too!"

Consider an initial meeting you have had with someone. Was humor used during this meeting phase? If so, what was your reaction? What type of humor was used? Did you want to spend more time with this person or get to know that person? If your answers were positive, you probably wanted to go to the next step, getting acquainted. If your conclusions were negative and you *had a choice*, you probably went straight to the final parting. It is important to acknowledge that there are some relationships we are not willing to sever. This could be a family member, a professional colleague or co-worker. This person may not be a favorite of yours but you may be obliged to maintain the relationship such as it is for personal or professional reasons.

Getting acquainted describes the process of spending time and learning more about the individual. In this phase, humor again can be used to keep things light, make both people feel comfortable and relaxed. As you spend time on this step, you further explore what types of humor are accepted by the other person. As this stage progresses, playfulness can enter into the relationship. This form of interplay stimulates comfortable laughter when there is mutual enjoyment; however, the reaction to playfulness can change when it is clearly a disguise for emotions we are unwilling to or do not know how to express. This occurs when one person says something that he or she laughs at but is not funny to the other or seems to be contradictory to what is being observed.

Teasing also emerges during this phase. *Teasing* is described as making fun of, mocking or harassing someone playfully (American Heritage Dictionary of English Language, 2003). It can be used to cover up feelings, be a method of revealing expectations and/or signal a level of intimacy either real or desired, such as one that is moving too fast. As relationships progress through the other stages, teasing often becomes more intimate (Sherman, 2003). A key concept here is to correctly assess the other person's sense of playfulness or humor. During the "Creative Humor at Work" seminar, a participant described a situation where she spent a couple of days with a man and they had a wonderful time. As a result of what appeared to be mutual enjoyment, she decided to make sure he remembered her after he left. She sent a bouquet of balloons to his work place, a school. She was laughing as she related, "I never heard from him again, but he told some friends he did not understand why I did that." This may be an example of an assessment of playfulness gone awry!

If the relationship continues, a *level of caring* develops. It could be simply liking the person enough to meet again. During this part of the process, humor can be used to mask feelings or to avoid expressing caring directly. While this can be achieved with gentle put-downs of self or others, more positive and straightforward ways to express caring are to give small gifts designed to elicit laughter about something learned during previous encounters. These can demonstrate thoughtfulness, sensitivity, playfulness, and caring. For example, someone knowing my passion for baseball sent me a tiny windup Ichiro doll that, when wound up and placed on a flat surface, runs around in circles and then falls down. Probably, only a person who has seen Ichiro play baseball for the Seattle Mariners or who is into baseball would know that this is not Ichiro behavior. For me, along with the irreverence of this gift which provided hilarity, I appreciated the thought and caring that was expressed. Another indirect method of communicating caring, one that can be misinterpreted or detrimental to relationships, is where one person mildly insults or belittles another. A friend volunteered an example:

> Many years ago, Linda invited a couple of her poetry group friends over for dinner. Included in her dinner were corn bread muffins which her friends raved about. At the end of the evening as her friends were leaving through the downstairs basement door, one of them noticed there was a sandbox in the basement for the kids to play that substituted corn meal for the sand, since it was lighter and easier to clean when spilled outside the box. Her friend commented on what a clever idea. I mentioned to her that I also thought it was a great idea and that in addition, it was very economical because once the kids were finished with it, Linda used it to make corn bread muffins. (R. Greenmun, personal communication, August 20, 2006)

A story from my brother is another example:

Remember Gavin's prayer to you over the phone when he was about four? "Come Lord Jesus do your best . . . " Then turning to me and said, "There's something wrong with Aunt Sandra!" I could hear you convulsed with laughter at the other end so in the interim I dutifully explained to him that this prayer only applied when his Aunt Sandra cooked.

In each case, the relationship between the primary persons is such that there was no insult intended or taken, so everyone understood and enjoyed the quip. This happens only where there is mutual respect and equal status. The same phenomenon occurs at celebrity roasts. The "roastee" laughs as hard as the "roaster" because regard is assured.

All long-term relationships eventually experience *conflict*, which can be overt as in loud arguments or covert using biting comments or sarcasm to hide anger, hurt, or frustration. In these situations, making fun of oneself or the other person by using disparaging humor is often utilized or perhaps we joke about what frustrates us or pretend to like what we obviously dislike. Humor may also escalate or terminate an argument. If used, humor can communicate expectations or social norms or may be perceived as a personal attack (Bippus, 2003).

Think about a time you were in an argument and the other person said something funny. Did you laugh? Or, did you get even angrier? If you did laugh, what happened to the argument and the anger? They probably evaporated. Now, think of the argument again. Did you decide not to laugh? Did the argument continue? Generally, if you want to continue an argument, you do not respond to a joke or anything funny; rather, you keep right on arguing. If you laugh and get distracted, it is only temporary and when you concentrate on the argument again, you resurrect those feelings. However, it is also possible that when you attend to the argument again, you will have a different perspective. The brief time out can change how you view the situation. Segal, Jaffe, DeKoven, and DeKoven (2006) advise that if you want to use playfulness in your relationship when addressing a difficult problem or conflict, it is important to assess whether you are "feeling calm, energetic, and lovingly connected to your partner and if your true intent is to communicate positive feelings, and whether your partner is calm and alert and in a good mood, open to hearing something self-critical" (p. 8). If your answer to these questions is an unqualified "yes," you will stand a greater chance of success in ending the argument or conflict.

A seminar participant related that she was furious with her husband and started chasing him around the dining room table, yelling at him. All of a sudden, she caught sight of the scene in the mirror over the sideboard, and, struck by the absurdity, began to laugh until tears ran down her cheeks. Her husband, of course, stopped and listened as she tried to explain the cause of her mirth. Since it is impossible to belly laugh and talk coherently, she made motions, he understood and he began to laugh as well. She reported that when they calmed down, she looked at him and said, "See, when you make plans that include me without checking first, I go crazy." They both laughed heartily again. She told the group after that he discussed plans with her. When he occasionally forgot, she never thought in the same way about not being consulted and never felt angry about it.

Sometimes conflict ends in a final parting, however, in long-term relationships it usually results in the next step, *separation*. Separation can last anywhere from moments to forever. One way humor can be used during the separation is to reflect on the argument from a distance, by seeking a different explanation for the conflict and/or its resolution. Children have a way of doing this. At dinner one night, Terry was not eating his broccoli. His mother reminded him once, and he still avoided his broccoli. His mother told him if he did not eat his broccoli he would have to go to his room until he decided to come out and finish his dinner including the broccoli. Again he left the broccoli alone. His mother took him crying to his room, shut the door, and came back to the table. Scarcely three minutes later, Terry returned, sat down, picked up his fork and said, "I've always liked broccoli better cold."

After a separation, when either of the parties is ready, sending funny cards, messages, gifts, or poems can signal that the conflict is resolved for that person and invite a *reconciliation*. One friend sent a bouquet of dead flowers to her boyfriend along with a note saying, "This is how I feel without you." The boyfriend called her upon receipt of the gift.

Sometimes using the *Humor Perspective* can force us to realize what may have been ignored and lead to a final separation or end the association as in this example. Colleen said:

> I was dating a brilliant man who, at one time, worked for US Intelligence. One night we were in his apartment on a sweltering, muggy Washington DC night. He had decided to open several windows to "let some air in." After he threw open all the windows and the room remained as hot as an oven, I suspected something was wrong and went to the window to see what might be amiss. I discovered the storm windows were still in place and closed. I asked if it wouldn't be more efficient if the storm windows were also raised. He agreed and proceeded to open them. What came next made me realize that I was superfluous to the relationship. When I asked, "Didn't you notice there wasn't a breeze?" He answered, "I thought I did." (C. Jensen, personal communication, 2006).

During the reconciliation phase of a relationship, humor is as a method of testing to see if the conflict is really over. It is a way to check to ask, "Am I still loved?" "Is he/she still angry?" or "Do I still care?" Teasing and being playful can also serve this purpose. If the other person laughs, whether the issue is resolved or not, the perception is that the argument is over, for now, and the next step in the relationship begins. In the broccoli-eating example, Terry thought it over and decided to come back and make a face-saving comment that resolved the broccoli conflict.

During this phase, called a *deeper level of caring*, playfulness and teasing become more intimate and reflect a deeper level of knowledge and involvement. By now each person in the relationship has learned more about the other and will know more about what makes the other person laugh so the gifts, cards, and interactions are more personal and intimate reflecting this deeper level of knowing. One close, long-time friend sent me an eraser when he learned I was writing this book! Pat Schwallie-Giddis remembered this story about her mother who she described as having a great sense of humor. She said her mother loved April Fool's Day. Her father bowled on a team every Wednesday night and always came home late. Pat's mother was a kindergarten teacher and was usually asleep when he arrived. Pat continued the story:

> Knowing how methodical he was, my mother knew he would tiptoe in, get into bed, roll over, and put his arm around her. One night, she took the stand used to hold her wig and very carefully laid it on the pillow next to his and used additional pillows to make it look like she was lying there asleep. As predicted, he saw the lights were off, carefully tiptoed into the bedroom, slipped off his clothes, quietly got into bed, rolled over and to put his arm around my mother. Much to his dismay, when he rolled over, the head fell to the floor with a thump. He screamed, "Jen, Jen, your head fell off!" At which time my mother who had been hiding in the closet came out laughing, saying, "April Fool." He did not think it was funny. After this incident, he always turned on the lights in the bedroom when he came home late. (P. Schwallie-Giddis, personal communication, (April 4, 2006)

During *final parting*, when a relationship is finished, humor can serve as a source of healing. As noted earlier, telling stories about someone who is no longer there serves to distance ourselves from those feelings and distract us. Again, laughter can be used to avoid expressing feelings of loss directly. That may not be as negative as it sounds. In times of loss, we all need some time out and a way to express our deep level of caring. Many families have had *Celebrations of Life* for the loved one who has died. This gathering of family and friends meeting in order to share memories of the deceased person may serve the same function as a wake and provides stories, both funny and not, for the grieving to use to distract themselves from the sadness they feel.

At my dear friend Allan's Celebration of Life, I told about one of my experiences with him. Allan was a brilliant, creative and wonderful friend. He was director of a statewide testing program for high school seniors. This test had a spatial relations test in the battery with items that showed a completed multi-dimensional figure followed by four possible responses, each laid out as a flat piece of paper with dotted lines. The person taking the test had to figure out which of the items, when folded on the dotted lines, would create the completed figure. One day, while talking to Allan, I learned he and I shared a common problem: we both had difficulty with spatial relations. We attempted to take the spatial relations test and discovered neither of us could complete even the easiest ones. Rather than getting frustrated, we took scissors and cut out each tiny figure with the dotted lines and folded them on the dotted lines to see which one was the correct answer. We must have laughed for several minutes as we played with

folding these tiny pieces of paper. Retelling this incident gave me a respite from
my grief over his death.

Artha tells about her father when he was in the early stages of Alzheimer's
disease and the family was unaware of this. They wanted to take him to Chicago
but he was reluctant to take the trip, so they tantalized him with the fact that they
would go to the Shedd Aquarium to see the Beluga Whales and also to see the
Rockettes perform. He finally agreed and the first stop was to see the Rockettes.
Sitting close to the front, with a chorus line of dancers doing their high kicks,
Artha's father asked loudly, "Where are the whales?" She said they all still
laugh about that as they remember and miss him.

At a recent OK Chorale rehearsal, Pamela confided that her mother had died
during the previous week. After condolences had been expressed, we continued
talking about other things. Just then another member arrived, sat down, and
asked Pamela how her mother was. She responded with tears in her eyes, "She is
wearing different clothes now." I piped up, "And wings." Pamela countered,
"Oh, no. I think where she is she will never be cold again." We all started laughing, Pamela hardest of all.

My friend Ann shared this story:

> In 2001, our mother unexpectedly died the month following her eightieth birth-
> day. After the funeral service, my siblings and I drove 75 miles north to trans-
> port Mom's ashes and funeral flowers to our hometown cemetery. That our
> family owns five cemetery plots results in ongoing confusion about who is bu-
> ried where and about who will ultimately lie in the unused plots. At the time of
> our mother's death, both grandparents and my father had died, using three of
> the five plots. Choosing cremation, my mother asked that her ashes be spread
> on our father's grave. In our fogged grief, we carefully spread the funeral flow-
> ers and my mother's ashes on our father's grave. After our preparations, solemn
> words and accompanying tears, one of us noticed that we were assembled
> around one of the empty graves. My brother glanced upward and quoted our fa-
> ther's favorite, loving-chiding sentiment: "Those dumb shit kids!" At that
> point, we collapsed in each other's arms in gasping laughter. (A. Blake, person-
> al communication, June 23, 2006)

After our father died, my brothers and I recalled funny stories about him
and since we all inherited his sense of humor, there were many of these. Mine
was about when my twin brother and I were about three and my father bet us
that he could jump higher than the house. After we bet him a penny, he said,
"You lose. The house can't jump."

Chapter 6

Humor Skills and Techniques

Would it not be fun if all of us could only see ourselves from a humorous perspective? Often, when we are our most serious, we are at our funniest but unable to see the absurdity of our actions. This chapter focuses on humor skills that can be useful to help you look at stressful situations from a *Humor Perspective*. Frequently, we are aware of the situations to which we react with stress or frustration. We can plan ahead by preparing a mental *Humor Kit* that can be accessed whenever it is needed to alleviate stressful reactions. For example, a friend described an incident where she and her partner had had a fight and were walking around Green Lake in Seattle to "cool off." It was a cold day and a flock of ducks were landing on the frozen lake. She began laughing as she described the ducks turning somersaults before finally skidding to a halt. She said both of them laughed heartily and after that they were able to talk through the issue that had started the argument. She indicated that since then whenever she finds herself getting upset, she thinks of how surprised those ducks were and how proud one of them appeared to be when it finally stopped!

This chapter identifies some humor skills and techniques that we can practice and include the results of using them in our Humor Kit. We can always use more practice at laughing at ourselves and some friends have contributed stories to demonstrate this skills. Creating metaphors, similes, puns, or verbal caricatures take some preparation but are useful to store in your Humor Kit. Finally, learning magic tricks and doing humor stretches are also valuable assets to add to your repertoire of stimulating laughter.

Laughing at Yourself

We all recall events that may have been embarrassing or not funny when they occurred but from our present perspective, being older and wiser, we recognize how funny they must have been at the time. Allen Klein (1989) advises laughing at yourself first before anyone else does. This gives others the opportunity to laugh with you, not at you.

Several women in my seminars have told stories about leaving a restroom with toilet paper caught in their panty hose, trailing behind them, and walking into a presentation or meeting. Every one of them was convulsed with laughter as they related the incident, even though at the time they may have been mortified by embarrassment. Think of a time when something similar happened to you. Stories like this belong in your mental Humor Kit, convenient for recalling at stressful times.

Some years ago at a professional conference, my committee of four decided to have a "different" sort of presentation for the banquet. When people finished eating, four of us, dressed like clowns, introduced the special entertainment, the audience. We asked the audience to think of something they did that might not have been funny at the time, but in retrospect became funny. The story had to be one that was not off color or putting someone down, and we asked that the story not be about someone else. We told them if they thought people might not laugh, they could request that we play a laugh tape (which we demonstrated) and if they wanted a standing ovation once they were finished they simply had to say, "I want a standing ovation." We assured them the ovation was guaranteed. After each story, the person was given a clown nose. For the rest of the conference, during the breaks, people would stop us "clowns" to say, "I forgot this one!" Throughout the rest of the meeting, people were telling stories and asking for standing ovations . . . and other presenters cooperated. It was a relaxed and fun group! One of the conferees said he was going to use that technique as part of admissions interviews and have candidates for admission into his university's Master of Arts in counseling program tell a funny story about themselves.

People who have had standing ovations that recognize outstanding efforts report that it feels good to be acknowledged by peers. In my seminar, participants are told that anytime they want a standing ovation while in the seminar, all they have to do is ask for one and they will get it. All they have to do is to stand up and say, "I want a standing ovation" and then enjoy the ovation they receive. They learn that we can give ourselves standing ovations in our imagination any time we do anything that we think deserves such acknowledgement and feel good about the accomplishment. This is similar to physically patting yourself on the back for your successes. These techniques are a humorous way to bolster self-esteem.

There are numerous examples of stories where people were able to laugh at themselves and these are some that have been shared by both friends and participants in the seminar. Two women shopping stopped in front of a clothed mannequin in a department store. One woman touched the front of the shirt and the pants fell off leaving the manikin bared from waist to the floor. Laughing uncontrollably, the two left the store to recover, but when they re-entered the store, began to laugh again. The saleslady came toward them with a puzzled look commenting, "I have to see what is so funny." She started laughing too and began to re-dress the manikin. As she was explaining about the clip in back that was holding up the pants, the clip broke and the pants fell again. It was several minutes before anyone could talk! The woman who had touched the shirt in the first place, observed, "Next time I will keep my hands to my self."

The secretary of our homeowners' association was getting minutes ready for our annual homeowners meeting when she found the following typo: "Anyone paying dues late are subject to a late feel [sic]." She could hardly describe the error to me, she was laughing so hard.

Jan, once a shipmate of mine, described an incident where she was being the "loyal, supportive, dutiful wife." Her husband was president of an organization and they often went to social gatherings where she met new people, so she tried a new technique for remembering the names: association. One woman she was introduced to and will forever remember was named Dil. Jan continued, "The next time I saw her, I marched right up to her, stuck out my hand and proudly said, "It's nice to see you again, Pickle." (J. Richardson, personal communication, May 25, 2006)

Sam Gladding (in press) contributed the following example of an ongoing situation about which he can laugh at himself now. He explained he grew up as a Baptist and at that time the Church expected people to keep track of time spent doing appropriate things like reading the Bible or being on time, as well as learning and reciting parts of the Bible. He described being a member of this church as challenging because he had to keep track of his good works and his witnessing activities. Every Sunday everyone completed a written form identifying how many times they read the Bible and did good things and Bible verses they had memorized.

Sam said he was fine with keeping records and memorizing Bible verses, but evangelism did not seem to be relevant "until one summer day when the weather and our minister both got hot." He was sitting with his family when the minister invited anyone who wanted to join the church to come up front with him. The congregation began to sing the hymn *Just as I Am*. After several verses had been sung and no one came forward, the minister asked the choir to sing "slowly and with feeling" while everyone else bowed their heads, hoping someone would come forward.

Suddenly, he called Sam and his friend Sandra to the front. Although they were shocked, they obeyed and Sam saw that Sandra was crying. He asked her what was wrong and she said, "I don't want to go to deepest darkest Africa as a missionary!" He agreed that this was not a goal for him either! However, obediently, they both went forward to stand where people could greet them. Since the call to come forward had taken so long, many people had already left but an elderly, very faithful member, "Miss Thelma," came forward and shook his hand enthusiastically, saying, "God bless you children." Sam remembered wishing he were somewhere else.

The story did not end there. No matter how old Miss Thelma was, she was always able to come to church and throughout the rest of his school career, whenever she saw Sam, she would ask how his study of Africa was going and proceed to ask him questions about Africa. He said he learned a lot about Africa during this time. He attended college out of town and every time he came home she would find him to see how his "missionary work" was going, assuming he was just home on vacation. He would always say he was being of assistance to those around him and that seemed to satisfy her as she smiled and walked away."

As a footnote, Sam explained:

> I think a striking aspect of the story for me is that in looking back I can see how I kept getting myself deeper and deeper into the situation because I refused to confess that I was not, nor had I ever been, nor was I ever going to be a missionary to Africa. I really thought the old lady, Miss Thelma, would probably pass on, i.e., die, and that I would be spared any embarrassment. But she just kept living and living and questioning and questioning, well . . . "Good Golly, Miss Molly." I had to study Africa or go down in infamy. So, I learned a lot about Africa, longevity (I really think I helped keep Miss Thelma alive), and human nature (my own). It was a farce and somewhat akin to a Shakespeare comedy except it was not as well written. Ironically I am now using that information I learned back during this almost-never-ending episode. On October 9th, I will take 60 counselors on a ten day trip to South Africa through People to People and ACA. You can bet I'll be laughing as I go and thank Miss Thelma for making me study geography, people, and customs I probably would have neglected otherwise. (S. Gladding, personal communication, September, 2006)

A friend, Marlys Olson, related this story about a friend of hers:

> My neighbor has a hard time putting on her socks due to a handicapping condition. She ordered a "sock assist" from a magazine, which consists of what looks like a sugar scoop without the handle and a long elastic loop. Her daughter came over and saw it on the bed. "What's that, Mom?" she asked. "A new senior citizen sex toy?" (M. Olson, personal communication, February, 2006).

A new minister demonstrated he was able to laugh at himself:

> There was a young new pastor in Artesia, New Mexico who was late to his first graveside service . . . the graveyard was not well marked and with him being new to this small town he drove all over the hills and desert for about an hour when he finally came upon a small sign leaning against some rocks reading, "Cemetery here." Upon entering the cemetery he saw two grave diggers filling in a hole, but no family members were around. After a moment of thinking through what he should do, he placed his vestments on, opened his bible, and began the graveside service. . . . The two grave diggers removed their hats and backed away in reverence. After the young pastor had finished and was walking back to his car, he heard one of the men say to other, "Zeke, ya think we otta' tell that young feller he just buried the septic tank?"

Creating Puns

Punning is a play on words. While punning has been called the lowest form of humor, many of us who use this method to laugh at life consider it to be one of the highest. Even though some offerings elicit groans as often as laughter, at least they get a reaction. Collecting puns can create its own entertainment. Greeting cards are one of the most used sources of puns. If you have spent any time around a large greeting card display, you have undoubtedly heard the chuckles as people searched for the appropriate one. Sometimes people will even share the card that caused the merriment. However, if we look around, our world can be another fruitful source. Some restaurants include puns in their menus. Denny's called their scrambled egg and ham sandwich, "Moon over my Hammy." Another specialty restaurant called their menu a "List of Pastabilities". A billboard overlooking a street in Seattle advertised cherry Yoplait Yogurt labeled, "My Cherie Amour" and another with Freud's picture on it alongside a new car carried the statement, "We were afreud [*sic*] you would miss our new car." During Christmas vacation, three of us were playing cards, with music playing in the background. At one point, a Mitch Miller tape started playing. I wondered if anyone remembered what his band was called. My cousin Jimmy responded, "Sons of Mitches."

Computers are fodder for some punsters, for example, Dracula saying, "One more byte and you will get it out of your system"; a computer operator has a chip on his/her shoulder"; or, "Computer operators do virus and sundry things." When I asked a friend to give me some medical puns to use with a hospital seminar in Boston, his instant response was:

> You could tell them, "You were 'panned' in Boston." Or tell them, "You would leave them in stitches." Or since you like to sing, how about singing Gonna Take a Sentimental Gurney home. (R. Rencken, personal communication, March 22, 1987)

Creating puns takes practice. One method of creating your own is by using a *Pun Wheel*. This technique is also called a *mind map*. To use this, you put the topic of your pun in the middle of a wheel with spokes radiating away from the middle and on each spoke place a related word. This can be accomplished on paper or in your head and when you have enough words, try to combine them in an unusual or funny way. Start with something simple. One student in a humor class did not like telemarketers, so she constructed a Pun Wheel with the word *telemarketer* in the center and came up with "Sales from the Script." I decided to use this technique on an afternoon when I found myself on the wrong side of a drawbridge when it was raised and subsequently got stuck. I was supposed to meet a friend and it was clear I was going to be late. Rather than becoming anxious about my tardiness in meeting my friend to go to the theater, I decided to use the time to create puns. I placed the word *automobile* mentally in the center of a Pun Wheel in my head and thought of related words: *tire, wheel, gas, ex-*

haust, brake, clutch, and so on. Then I put them together: I am tired, retired, semi-retired, exhausted, and all clutched up. When I used this example in future seminars, helpful participants added a few more, such as, "You were out fueling around," "That was the brakes," and, "You were wheelie wheelie mad." At the time, I was so engrossed in my punning, I forgot where I was until I became aware that cars were going around me . . . I was now the traffic jam! Since Seattle has lots of water and many bridges, I have found this tool helpful many times.

Still another example of using the Pun Wheel was using a card with a picture of a beaver sitting on a log that had "I love you" carved on it. Beaver would be in the center, with spokes containing the words *carve, tail, teeth, tooth, animal, pelt, build, chew, chip, fur, water, dam, wood, mud, flat,* and so on. Possibilities to finish the phrase "I love you . . . " are:

- . . . that's the long and tail of it.
- . . . it's the tooth.
- . . . I've been wanting to tail (tell) you fur a long time.
- . . . a chip thrill.
- . . . woodn't you believe me?
- . . . furever, untail the 12th of never.
- . . . I be fur you, let's beaver each other.

Another pun-creating activity is adapted from Joel Goodman's "Laughter and Creativity" workshop (Goodman, 1984). I have used this technique successfully with large groups of 50 or more people. Participants are instructed to throw two things they had brought with them to the seminar onto the middle of the floor and then look at all of the "treasures" and pick up two or three and put them together in "punny" ways. Among the responses that have been generated was the one woman who took a ball and stuffed it under her long sweater which made her look pregnant and said, "I'm having a ball." We had barely recovered from that when another woman took off her prosthesis, shook it and said, "Shake a leg." Other responses have been: "comb, comb over change" for a handful of change with two combs on top; "time flies," said while tossing a watch to someone; "heart and sole," said with a shoe to someone's chest; "clip joint," said with a paper clip to the elbow; and "you are making a spectacle of yourself," referring to glasses. Once participants get warmed up, even the most reluctant join the parade of "groaners."

If punning is not your style for creating humor, you can find some on the Internet. Here are some sample puns gathered from the Chet Meeks' (2006) Page of Puns on Internet:

- What does an Olympic fencing hopeful do at noon each day? Leaves his office and goes out to lunge.

- A new seminar topic: "Everything You Always Wanted to Know About Phobias and Were Afraid to Ask."
- If the cops arrest a mime, do they tell him he has the right to remain silent?
- For people who like peace and quiet . . . a phoneless cord.
- If a parsley farmer is sued, do they garnish his wages?
- Cole's Law: thinly sliced cabbage.

Meeks published this one on his site too:

The Seattle Symphony was performing Beethoven's Ninth Symphony. Toward the end of this symphony, there are pages and pages where the basses do not play. That section decided rather than sitting idly on stage, they would all exit and return in time to resume playing and they did so. Once offstage, one of the basses suggested they go to the bar across the street for a drink. After the second drink, someone thought they should return to Performance Hall. One of others explained that there was still time, because he had tied a string around the score and the conductor would have to slow down to untie the string and so they had time for one more. After the third drink, they hurried across the street and as they came on stage, they saw that the conductor was furious. As well he should have been: it was the bottom of the ninth, the score was tied and the basses were loaded. (Meeks, 2006)

Additional contributions:

1. Evidence has been found that William Tell and his family were avid bowlers. However, all the Swiss league records were unfortunately destroyed in a fire. Thus we'll never know for whom the Tells bowled.

2. A man rushed into a busy doctor's office and shouted "Doctor! I think I'm shrinking!!" The doctor calmly responded, "Now, settle down. You'll just have to be a little patient."

3. A marine biologist developed a race of genetically engineered dolphins that could live forever if they were fed a steady diet of seagulls. One day his supply of the birds ran out. So he had to go out and trap some more. On the way back, he spied two lions asleep on the road. Afraid to wake them, he gingerly stepped over them. Immediately, he was arrested and charged with transporting gulls across sedate lions for immortal porpoises.

4. Back in the 1800s the Tates Watch Company of Massachusetts wanted to produce other products and, since they already made the cases for pocket watches, decided to market compasses for the pioneers traveling west. It turned out that although their watches were of finest quality; their compasses were so bad that people often ended up in Canada or Mexico rather than California. This, of course, is the origin of the expression, "He who has a Tates is lost!" (T. McKiel, personal communication, March 10, 2006)

Verbal Caricatures, a Form of Exaggeration

Exaggeration can be expressed in several ways. The most common is the *caricature*. Cartoonists create a humorous image of a person by exaggerating a particular physical characteristic in order to make people laugh or smile. Another form of caricature is *verbal exaggeration*. Using this humor tool, we can create verbal caricatures making fun of behavioral traits. Select a behavior that is aggravating, create a funny name that exaggerates that behavior (or create an exaggerated picture of that behavior in your head) and keep it handy in your Humor Kit. Keep in mind these refer to specific behaviors, not people, although it is an individual who exhibits the behavior. For example, if whining irritates you, create a name for that behavior that exaggerates it to the point of the ridiculous and to which you respond to the name with a smile or chuckle (e.g., Tammy Whinette). When you are confronted with that behavior, your own or another person's, tune into your verbal caricature and distract yourself. Doing this puts some distance from the behavior that you dislike and allows you to look at it from another perspective, the *Humor Perspective*.

As part of a program for the American Counseling Association's Governing Council, a colleague and I created a series of caricatures exaggerating behaviors one might find in a large organizational meeting, behaviors that can annoy or cause stress. Among our creations were: *Lady Chatterly, Phil E. Buster* or *Gwen Onanon*, for someone who talks all the time; *Dr. Robert* or *Dr. Roberta Ruler*, for someone who only sees black and white and has memorized *Roberts Rules of Order*; *Noah Tall*, for someone who "knows" everything; and *Dee Fear*, for someone who does not listen. Other verbal caricatures contributed from various seminar participants who practiced with this activity: *Hiram N. Firam, Tim Buck II, Polly Ester Doublenitz, Ida Wanna, Les B. Petty,* and *Bertha Buttinsky*. In each case, the behaviors are exaggerated to help bring humor to a situation that could create stress. We all have buttons, that when pushed, cause us frustration. If we can tap into our Humor Kit and remember the caricatures "stored" there, we can give ourselves some distance and look at these behaviors differently and maybe even laugh rather than become aggravated.

Still another type of verbal exaggeration is simply to overemphasize whatever bothers you until it is ridiculous to you. Create special awards like a "Terse Award for Brevity" for someone who talks a lot (you never have to present it). Keep in mind that if you ever present these awards, be sure the recipient has laughed at this behavior in the past.

Another method using exaggeration that has worked successfully in the Creative Humor at Work seminar is to have small groups of people write a "stress or aggravations song" about their complaints. They start with a warm-up phase in buzz groups related to nonsensical topics, then proceed to create the "performance piece." Also, they are instructed to decide on a name for their group so they can be properly introduced for their performance. This is done in five minutes or less. While many people insist they cannot sing, a group as small as three people have been able to perform their song successfully. These creations are received by the rest of the participants with cheering, loud applause and even louder standing ovations.

Some memorable performances include one group standing on a table and pantomiming a rock band playing. When they finished, they introduced themselves as "The Silent Minority." Some of the more frequently used melodies are *My Favorite Things, Row, Row, Row your Boat*, and *Three Blind Mice* but occasionally there are more ambitious contributions. A group of Boeing managers enjoyed success using *Partridge in a Pear Tree*. All I remember of that one is that the fifth day of Christmas was something like, "On the fifth day of Christmas, management gave to me . . . five additional projects." It seemed to work for them!

Albert Ellis (1987), a master at exaggeration, composed songs years ago as part of his therapeutic approach, and participants have reported the results of their songwriting experience as no less therapeutic than Ellis'songs. While his are about psychological issues, these songs come from the here and now of the participants.

Here is a recent example from a Seattle group:

The Complainers (Sung to the tune of *Do, Re, Mi*)
Rains a pain, a great big pain
Those who never give you praise,
George the moron at the helm
Time forever running short
We work for money never seen
Kids and husband never clean,
Life is just one long hard dream
And I live on lean cuisine.

Years after first doing this activity, Don Glabe, a retired elementary counselor, described using this technique in psychological/counseling staffing meetings. He imagined each participant was part of an opera and he transposed everything that was said into an operatic melody. Here is his story:

THE OPERA OF M.D.T. MEETINGS

As a counselor I attended "multidisciplinary team meetings" each week at the two elementary schools to which I was assigned. Sometimes the comments shared in these sessions began to seem so familiar and repetitious that I drifted in my attention. I started to imagine the proceedings as an opera, with each voice sharing their information and pleading their case with operatic zeal.

The Psychologist, Tenor, "These obtained standard scores do not meet the state and district requirements for a Special Placement."

Teacher, Mezzo Soprano, "Surely there must be something for this student, He is the most difficult I have seen in all my 15 years of teaching. If something isn't done, I just mean something must . . . "

Nurse, Soprano, "Was there some birth trauma? Yes I think the umbilical cord was wrapped and wrapped around this poor child's neck that may be relevant. Birth trauma, and umbilical cord very, very relevant."

Principal, Basso, "Are you sure your scores don't qualify? Really now we need some help for this student and this teacher. What about Professional Judgment?"

Psychologist, Tenor, "They are not my scores, they are the student's scores and they do not, do not, qualify this student for special funding services. However If there is medical involvement that may be another thing. Yes Professional Judgment could be used."

Teacher, Nurse, Principal, Psychologist, Unison, "Yes, And Professional Judgment will save the day."

Counselor, Baritone, "Wait, have you considered cultural and home conditions?"

Teacher, Nurse, Principal, Psychologist, Unison, "Yes, And Professional Judgment will save the day."

Well anyway this little fantasy helped me through many of these meetings and I do maintain that the decisions that were ultimately made were quite educationally sound. (D. Glabe, personal communication, May 24, 2006)

Writing poems about life's distresses also can be helpful. Sometimes it is the little things that finally get to us. I do not know if men encounter this in restrooms but a few years ago I decided to look at the phenomenon of a woman leaving the toilet seat liner on the seat when she leaves the restroom stall. I wrote the following *Ode to a User* and considered taping it to doors of restrooms around the world.

> It's so nice of you to think of me
> When you cover where my butt will touch.
> I'd rather you did something else, you see.
> Please. Crumple, toss in the toilet and flush.

Or a way to combat frustration in families:

> Kids are frustrating, please believe me.
> They get noisy and they race through the house
> With dirty clothes, messy rooms, and then glued to TV
> I can see they take after my spouse.

Metaphors and Similes

Metaphors or *similes* are also tools to help us look at situations from new perspectives. They communicate a unique meaning or feeling of a situation, a meaning that might be lost in a different type of explanation. Consider a quote by John Boehner after he was elected as House of Representatives majority leader, "I feel like the dog who caught the car" (*Time*, February 13, 2006). Metaphors are deeply embedded in our culture: baseball, banking, cooking, weather, law, fishing, and so on. Examples of these metaphors: *striking out, foul play, fluid assets, floating a loan, a fine kettle of fish, cooking one's goose, scattered sunshine* (for Seattle weather), *storm of controversy, grilling the witness,* and *a fine kettle of fish.* You have heard the terms, *rug rat, couch potato,* and *road hog.* Each of the phrases describe in a few words what might take many more to describe.

Also, metaphors can be used as a simple diagnostic tool to get an idea of one's state of mind or, as in the above example, they can express feelings without getting lost in language. Like a picture, a metaphor (or simile) can be worth a thousand words. "Life is like a trip through the Milky Way, smooth sailing with occasional explosions when a new star is born" carries a note of hope while "Life is (like) a bowl of lemons and you don't have the sugar for lemonade" or, "In the banquet of life I feel like a leftover" express a sense of helplessness. Describing life, work, problems, situations, or behaviors as metaphors can give us a new perspective and possibly even make us laugh, thus creating the psychological distance often needed to help us think in new ways.

Creating metaphors can be made simpler by using *metaphorical stems.* (Gladding, 2006), He categorizes these stems into:

- warm up metaphors (*I feel . . . , I eat like . . .* or *When I'm mad, I'm like . . .*),
- object metaphors (*What object would you be if you had a choice?*)
- house metaphors (*What kind of house would you be if you had a choice?*)
- animal metaphors (*What kind of animal would you be?*)
- color metaphors (*What color are you?*)
- lyrical metaphors (*favorite line from a song*). For example, the following words from the song *The Rose* reflect hope, " . . . in the Winter far beneath the bitter snows / Lies the seed that with the sun's love, in the spring becomes the rose" (Gladding, 2006, p. 1).

In each case, the metaphor helps identify feelings and meanings for clients.

Another method for creating metaphors comes from Ferguson, Coleman, and Perrin (1990). Using this method, write one word on each of fifty note cards. Most of these have to be concrete nouns, while a small number can be adjectives or abstract nouns. No verbs or adverbs are allowed. The words should be interesting or important to you. Once the cards are completed, shuffle them and pick out two random selections and try to connect them with the word "is." In order to create a metaphor, the two words must be contradictory. While this does take time, you will no doubt find at least one metaphor that will make you smile or laugh.

In an interview for National Public Radio, I was asked to give an example of a metaphor. Using a simile I had prepared earlier, I responded, "Dieting is like being the guest of honor at a cannibal luncheon and you are the only one who does not get to eat." The interviewer observed that this was very negative and I responded, "Yes, but this is how I feel about dieting." That one never made it on the air.

Humor Stretches and Magic

In my two-day seminars, participants are asked to do a *humor stretch*. A humor stretch is defined as the participant doing something he or she has not done before and so is somewhat of a risk, is funny to the individual and is not hurtful or demeaning to anyone. Three graduate students received the assignment and during their dinner hour, stopped at a Circle K store. They then went to a restaurant for dinner. The first one ordered a hamburger from the server, then pulled a package of hamburger buns out of a bag and asked if the chef could use one of those buns. The server explained the chef had buns and probably would not like to use anyone else's. The student continued to press by saying he had eight buns and did not eat hamburgers often so they would go stale. The enterprising server explained again why the chef would not use "anyone else's buns" and suggested the student freeze his buns individually and then he could thaw them one at a time. She moved to the next person who ordered iced tea and asked for it to be served in a pitcher along with shot glasses, saying, "When we were kids, drinking out of shot glasses made us feel grownup." The server agreed to do so. The third student ordered and asked if the server could bring salt in packets like those served on airplanes. When told there was salt on the table, the student observed, "Yes, but it just doesn't taste the same." They came back to the seminar and related this story. While these requests may sound like they inconvenienced the server, she seemed to take them in stride. The next morning the students added a post script. They had returned to the restaurant after the seminar that night and ordered a pitcher of beer. They had the same server and she brought the pitcher of beer with three shot glasses! If their earlier fun really was at the expense of the server, she got them back.

When I was doing the humor stretch in Germany, one participant borrowed two clown suits and two sets of juggling scarves, and in the middle of a very large crowd at an outdoor festival, she and her daughter wore the clown suits and juggled. Neither had ever done this before so it was a risk for them. The mother reported they both had a great time and provided entertainment for the crowd. They had to assume this from the smiles and laughter they saw and heard since the comments were in German.

Others who have participated in the humor stretch activity reported what one person described as a profound experience. This man had a two-year-old son and thought it would be fun to dress like a clown for him. He took the clown paraphernalia home and put it on. He said when he walked into the room in the clown suit, wig, and red nose, his son started screaming and did not stop until he took all the clown gear off and showed his child it was Daddy. Then he re-dressed with his son helping him and the child began laughing. As he told this story, the participant had tears in his eyes as he relived the experience of having terrified his son. Many of us tend to generalize our own reactions to experiences to others, and in this case, he associated his experience with clowns being funny and assumed his son would react the same way he did. He vowed never again to assume that he knew what would be fun for his child.

Magic tricks can also be a stretch for some people. There is the risk of per-forming the trick incorrectly and/or being the focus of everyone's attention. A simple "trick" to start with was one taught by David Copperfield at the "Healing Power of Laughter and Play" workshop (1984). This "trick" required us to hold a pencil lying across the V-shaped crook between our thumb and forefinger as the palms of our hands faced each other an inch apart. Then, we crossed one thumb over the other and rotated them, moving the pencil so it remained within the crook but was on the underside of our hands which were now parallel to each other facing the floor. After a few tries, we all mastered this "trick." After-wards he showed us a video where he taught this "trick" to children with hand injuries. We could see they were so engrossed with accomplishing the trick suc-cessfully, that some of them actually moved their hands and did not report pain. The look on their faces as they manipulated the pencil was joyful and touching to watch.

In a university humor class I taught, students were required to learn a magic trick to demonstrate to the class. The magic feats were varied and each "magi-cian" looked pleased as if doing this was fun. One that stands out because of the outcome was one where Marie asked her daughter, Jessica, to be her assistant. She was going to do a trick wherein she made her daughter disappear behind two bedsheets. Two other students, facing each other, held up the sheets, parallel to each other, one sheet in each hand. Jessica got between the sheets, and Marie said her magic words and told the sheet holders to drop the outside sheet. They did so and we saw Jessica's rear end disappearing under the back sheet. Of course we were not supposed to see her disappear! Totally in control, Marie said she was going to make her assistant reappear and asked her helpers to raise the front bedsheet again. Then she said some more magic words and told them to drop the front sheet once more and we saw Jessica emerge from under the back sheet. Unfortunately Jessica was supposed to have disappeared and reappeared *before* the sheet was dropped! Somehow the real magic occurred when the trick went awry! Marie received a loud and boisterous standing ovation for her trick and was laughing as hard as the rest of us.

Chapter 7

Creative Humor at Work:
Using the *Humor Perspective*

Looking at the world with humor, laughter, and play helps make life stresses easier to manage. This chapter discusses useful applications of humor in serious situations, such as illness, long-distance non-custodial parental communication, and war.

Humor and Illness

There are many stories about people utilizing humor with seriously ill patients (Cousins, 1989). Joshua, Cotroneo, and Clarke (2005) describe two types of humor found in oncology: *spontaneous* and *prepared*. The first is part of an interaction between the doctor and the patient and the second is included in written information given to the patient to help them see the "lighter side" of cancer care (p. 645). The authors indicated humor is of "great importance in oncologic care" and explained it is a viable defense mechanism but they cite a lack of references in medical literature. They wondered if this was because humor is not an acceptable subject for study or if using humor might be harmful to patients and concluded trust and timing are critical when using any type of humor. They suggest using "gentle humor . . . inviting the patient to laugh" (p. 646) and, if the person does not laugh, to stop using this tactic.

Humor can help the patient take a break from the pain, the worry and the fear of being seriously ill. When we laugh, we affirm our aliveness. Also, if we are the patient and we can laugh, it can be helpful to those who love us who are concerned about, worrying or fearing the outcome of our illness. Some personal examples help bring this into focus. Betty has terminal lung cancer. She lives at home and that is where she wishes to stay. She told me she has lived a long and good life and wants to enjoy what is left of it so has continued to smoke and to have her daily cocktail. When she is able, she goes to the casino to gamble and even went on a hunting trip with her close friend, Marleen. She goes to the doctor only when the pain is so bad her current medication does not help. In the meantime, as a lifelong joke teller, she decided to leave a legacy. She sat for two and a half hours, told one joke after another, and videotaped the entire performance. When she talked about doing that, she was smiling and chuckling. She continues to tell jokes even on days when she does not feel well.

An emergency medical worker who responded to a 911 call for Betty related how she persists in her use of humor. The ambulance was called because Betty was in severe pain from constipation. One of the technicians was interviewing her and asked if there was anything to which she was allergic. Betty responded, "Obviously to sh*t."

Even though hope and positive attitudes help people fight illness and some of those lose the battle, Cousins (1989) observed:

> There is something about making a supreme effort in coping that gives meaning to life, even under the most trying and poignant circumstances. This holds true not just for the patient but for members of the family who desperately need evidence of a total response to serious challenge. (Cousins, 1989, pp. 102–103)

Betty's friend, Marleen, will attest to this as she sees her dear friend in pain. Betty's humor helps both of them.

Another friend, Allan, was seriously ill and always loved to laugh. He dubbed the books I brought him "A Traveling Laugh Kit." The kit contained several books: *Calvin and Hobbes*, the *Journal of Irreproducible Results, Anatomy of an Illness,* and *Peace, Love and Healing.* As we talked on the telephone, he would often bring up one of the funny things he remembered and laugh again with me. He returned the kit so someone else could benefit from it. Cousins (1989) and Klein (1989) both advise people to take jokes, cartoons, and funny gifts to patients instead of the traditional flowers.

An article on the Internet, "Humor and Mental Health: Using Humor to Cope with Stress" (2005) describes a housebound patient with numerable physical problems. For a period of time he was very negative about his life, complained about his limitations and seemed to have given up hope. At one point, the in-home caregiver was replaced by one who had a "good sense of humor." The article reported the new caretaker interacted with her patient in a playful manner and his behavior changed. He became lighter and began to tell jokes. The author credited the caregiver with bringing out her father's playfulness and helping him improve his quality of life (p. 3).

I was invited to talk about humor with a group of caregivers of Alzheimer patients. One man could not find anyone to stay with his wife so he brought her along. I was talking about laughing at yourself as a survival skill and the group was just not buying what I was saying. They were trying to understand but it was not working. One person said, "If we do that we are laughing at someone we love." I tried again but knew what I thought I was saying was not what they were hearing. About that time, the Alzheimer patient said, "Listen to her. She knows what she is talking about." Everyone looked startled, a few smiled and they began to discuss the merits of using humor as they interacted with their loved one as long as this could not be construed as making fun of them. They all knew she was an Alzheimer patient and her spontaneous outburst seemed to break down a barrier that I had not been able to get through.

In the early 70s I was hospitalized for tests. My roommate was a woman with serious heart problems. As we talked, she mentioned she was scared about the tests she would undergo and with nothing to do, she was finding it difficult to not think about the upcoming tests. I offered to teach her to play a card game. She agreed. As we played we laughed again and again. Finally, a nurse came to our door and apologetically said, "I'm sorry I have to close your door. We don't hear a lot of laughter up here and it's a little noisy for the other patients." She and I continued our game and laughter behind the closed door as she visibly relaxed. She thanked me for distracting her, telling me that she was dreading the upcoming tests and found it refreshing to be able to have fun playing cards and not think of them for awhile.

Times have changed. Today, it appears more hospitals and medical personnel are believers that laughter, although noisy, is infectious. Many hospitals have instituted "Humor Rooms" based on the belief that tension in both patients and staff is reduced through laughing. These rooms contain funny videos, funny books, cartoons, movies, anything that could tickle the funnybone. Other hospitals have introduced a rolling "Humor Cart" that visits patients' rooms. They contain humorous books, audio and video tapes, games, cartoons, and so on. These are often run by volunteers from the community. Some hospitals have set aside a room dedicated to fun and games for ambulatory patients. St. Joseph's Hospital in Houston has made believers out of staff who maintain humor leads to shorter hospital stays for many. In a hospital in New York, there is a full-time coordinator of humor whose job is to make humor available to patients who wish to laugh. Berk and Bittman (1999) developed a humor instrument called "SMILE (Subjective Multidimensional Interactive Laughter Evaluation)", built on the notion that all of us have a preference for specific types of humor. Patients answer questions about how they feel and the types of humor they enjoy, and when finished "receive what Dr. Berk calls a 'humor prescription'—a detailed list of suggested reading materials, videotapes, and audiotapes that the person might enjoy" (Berk & Bittman, 1999, p. 1).

Gascon (2004) has developed a list describing the benefits of using humor when ill:

12 Things Humor Gives Where Illness Lives

1. Helps the person step back from their illness.
2. Gains perspective and a breath of fresh air.
3. Shows them that there is more to life than just physical disabilities.

4. Opens minds to realities that are fun, joyous and light.
5. Makes them smile.
6. Achieves states that are tranquil, flowing and worry-free.
7. Validates the fact that although someone may be seriously ill or in the process of dying, at the moment, they are alive!
8. Involves everyone in the conversation.
9. Insulates against loneliness and fear.
10. Is a sign of approval, caring, compassion and connection.
11. Loves them with lightness and joy.
12. Lifts the spirit and speeds recovery!

(Gascon, 2004, p. 1)

Non-custodial Parent Maintaining Long-distance Relationships with Children

An area where little has been written is how non-custodial parents who live a significant distance from their children can use humor to maintain contact and connection. Often single non-custodial parents find themselves living a distance away from their children and are not able to be physically available. What can a parent do to maintain the relationship long-distance? Articles and books have been written on the topic of non-custodial parenting and several stress the importance of listening, a critical component of the relationship. I remember flying home from San Diego after teaching a class on child counseling. On the plane I sat next to two unrelated children, a boy and a girl, both no older than six. I stuffed my tote bag under the seat and my puppets, from the program Developing Understanding of Self and Other (DUSO), were visible. The little boy kept looking at those puppets and finally his curiosity got the better of him. He asked, "What are those?" I explained they were puppets. He wondered what I did with them. I responded, "I use them to teach grownups how to talk with children." His response was immediate, "Wow. Would you talk to my dad?" Listening and communicating are very important and, since laughter breaks down barriers, humor can facilitate the relationship and communicate positive messages across the distance.

My nephew, Gavin, lived his first 12 years separated from his father by several hundred miles so my brother, Ed, created humorous ways to maintain his connection and communicate with his son. Of course there were frequent phone calls and intermittent visits, but much of their contact was engineered by my brother through the mail.

One method he used was to write a question at the top of the page and the bottom of the page would have little doors that could be opened, glued onto the paper. Something was written behind each door. One letter might have the question: "What do you get from a spoiled cow?" Behind one door might be, "Wrong, really cold," another might be, "Warm," a third could be, "Warmer" and the fourth, "Spoiled milk" or, "Call for the correct answer," Other examples of what was behind the tabs were: Tab A—"You were supposed to tell your Mom the answer first, grubby little kid!! Do that and <u>THEN</u> check Tab B"; Tab B—"HEY PUT THAT BACK YOU ARE LETTING IN THE LIGHT!!! Signed, A. Germ."; Tab C might have a stick of gum; and Tab D might be written backward so he had to use a mirror. Occasionally there was a fill-in-the-blank from a list of words, a poem about Gavin, always some type of surprise.

One month my nephew received the following instructions to the tab game: "Gavin, open TAB A to see something that you can see in Juneau but I can't see in Fairbanks." The tab covered a hole in the paper so he would be looking at his feet or something else in the house. Ed reported this kept Gavin looking forward to the letters, and he knew his father was thinking about him. Usually, my brother received a telephone call soon after the letter arrived that started with "Papa" or, when he was older, "DaaaaD!" One time Ed gave Gavin a list of German words to learn, then wrote, "Ich leibe dich mein sohn, du bist ein gutter kind. Leibe, Father." The rest of the letter said, "Gavin, once you get this figured out write it down and send it to me. If you are right, I'll send you some jerky. I love you my son, you are a good child. Love, Father" (E. Meggert, Personal communication, February 24, 2006). He called his dad with the correct response, was very proud of himself and made a comment something like, "Dad. You gave me the answer!" His pleasure was two-fold: he figured out what his father said and thought his dad did not realize what he had done.

Ed wrote a short book for Gavin called a *Big and Little Book for Gavin*. There was a picture of a big gorilla and one of a little gorilla below with the caption, "Big Gorillas love Little Gorillas"; a picture of a big creature with a picture of a little creature next to it with the caption, "Big Creatures love Little Creatures"; a picture of a big penguin with a little penguin leaning against him with the caption "Big Penguins love Little Penguins"; a picture of a big mummy with a small mummy below and a caption "Big Mummies love Little Mummies"; and a big sun with a smile adjacent to a little sun with a smile and the caption "Father suns love Son suns". The last page had a drawing of an eye in one corner. Opposite is "Love" and the bottom, a large U with "Dad" under it. Gavin got that one too. Ed said he always sent one of these letters with the monthly check and hoped Gavin would eventually understand that he was helping to support him financially as well.

While Gavin was visiting, Ed would wake him up with riddles and if he responded accurately there was a prize. One example was, "Amorous amphibian sought passionate association," the answer for which is "Froggy went a Courtin'," a song Gavin had heard many times as he was growing up. Or, what do you call a pig that loses its voice? Answer: Disgruntled. After Gavin came to live with his father to "help" him with doing chores, taking medicine or doing homework, my brother would place a candy on top of whatever Gavin was going to use to complete the task. Eventually my brother would ask him if he had vacuumed, done his homework, and so on. Gavin never lied but might say, "What do you think?" The response was, "I don't have to think, I know" and my brother would go to the vacuum cleaner or homework book and find the candy and pop it into his mouth. Gavin could never be sure when the candy would appear.

Gavin lost a tooth when he was 10 and received the following application for a "Tooth Replacement Grant":

APPLICATION FOR TOOTH REPLACEMENT GRANT

Dear Mister Meggert;

It has come to our attention that you have lost and may be considering replacing a tooth. Our institution has been involved with various aspects of the tooth industry for centuries including financing replacements. The tooth you recently lost blue booked at $3.00 less than cost so you are currently in arrears to Tooth Fairy, Inc. (TFI) for that amount. However, the good news is you may be qualified for a grant for the replacement of this tooth which would cover not only the amount owed but leave a bit left over for those unexpected expenses such as toothpaste, braces, etc.

Please read the following categories in step one and check the appropriate one(s) to see if you are qualified for the grant program. Then go on to step two.

STEP 1

You have been your present age less long than you were your previous age.

The total of the 2 digits in your age equals 3 or less.

STEP 2 – Check each box that applies

☐ I brush my teeth twice each day

☐ I brush my teeth once per day

☐ I brush my teeth once every other day

☐ I use mouth wash

☐ Girls comment on how white my teeth look

☐ I never chew on high wear items such as spitzer scoresheets with my teeth

☐ I never eat candy

☐ I never eat ice cream

☐ I need my teeth because I smile a lot

☐ My mouth gets the most use of any part of my body

When finished please place this application under your pillow. The results of this application will be scored and the Duly Appointed Determiner will determine the amount of the grant if any. If you qualify the remittance will be sent in the usual manner UTP (Under The Pillow).

I agree with the terms and conditions of this contract.

Gavin M. Meggert

While humor is not the only thing that keeps long-distance relationships alive, it can be a helpful tool in maintenance. In this case, it made such an impression on Gavin that he eagerly looked forward to being with his father because he had learned he would have fun. Of course, the humor was part of the entire range of communication tools that were used with him.

Humor in Wartime

War is not funny. One of the things that isolate us from the horror, fear and grief of war is to ridicule what we can. Laughter serves as a buffer against pain. The important thing to remember is in order to laugh at something this serious, you must be a member of the group. Just as other professions use humor to provide a means to distance pain, so do those in war zones. As with medical personnel, often humor is specific to their experience and anyone not in that situation might judge the wisecrack or joke as not funny or insensitive, but for the person in the situation, it serves to alleviate the distress. Many jokes and cartoons about the war are written by people not in the situation, and who may not fully understand what actual warfare is like. If these were created by someone who was fighting in the war, it might not be funny to us because we did not experience the situation and only know of it by written or oral descriptions. In one sense, people in like situations create their own language of humor.

In Germany last November, a military officer, who was going to be deployed to Iraq the following month, attended the "Creative Humor at Work" seminar I conducted. I later emailed him and received the following response:

We got here at the beginning of January when it was still wet and rainy. Yep, it rains here, and everything floods. The sand is like a fine powder that turns to mud as soon as it rains. It stopped raining in February, I think. The hot weather is here for another month and then it will start to cool off. We had a small break in the heat this past week when it only got to 105–109 for the high. That's

about 3-6 degrees cooler than normal. While that doesn't seem like a big difference, we could feel it. It's still hot, just not as hot.

I ate lunch today with a guy I was stationed with four years ago. We were talking about all the people we worked with and some of the funny things they did.
He made the comment that things that weren't funny eight months ago are funny now because he's been here for eight months. He got here before I did so he
gets to leave sooner.

I think everyone in my office is a believer of "it only has to be funny to you to
be helpful." There is a lot of laugher here, so that's a good thing." (K. Klopcic,
personal communication, March, 24, 2006)

He noted he received this from the Chaplain with his unit:

There were two boys, Timothy Murphy and Antonio Secola, whose lives parallel each other in amazing ways. In the same year Timothy was born in Ireland,
Antonio was born in Italy. Faithfully they attended parochial school from kindergarten through their senior year in high school.

They took their vows to enter the priesthood early in college, and upon gradua-
tion, became priests. Their careers had come to amaze the world, but it was
generally acknowledged that Antonio Secola was just a cut above Timothy
Murphy in all respects. Their rise through the ranks of Bishop, Archbishop and
finally Cardinal was swift to say the least, and the Catholic world knew that
when the present Pope died, it would be one of the two who would become the
next Pope.

In time the Pope did die, and the College of Cardinals went to work. In less
time than anyone had expected, white smoke rose from the chimney and the
world waited to see whom they had chosen.

The world, Catholic, Protestant and secular, was surprised to learn that Timothy
Murphy had been elected Pope!

Antonio Secola was beyond surprise. He was devastated, because even with all
of Timothy's gifts, Antonio knew he was the better qualified. With gall that
shocked the Cardinals, Antonio Secola asked for a private session with them in
which he candidly asked, "Why Timothy?"

After a long silence, an old Cardinal took pity on the bewildered man and rose
to reply. "We knew you were the better of the two, but we just could not bear
the thought of the leader of the church being called Pope Sicola. (K. Klopcic,
personal communication, June, 25, 2006)

Kevin has returned from Iraq safely. He sent many examples of humor used in
Iraq and thoughtfully explained the meaning of some of the terms. These contributions poignantly reflect the horror and danger with which army field person-

nel are faced with daily. One of his contributions expresses the resignation about
the reality of their situation:

> Question: What do the Easter Bunny, Osama Bin Laden and Santa Claus have
> in common with *R & R* (rest and relaxation)?
> Answer: They are all figments of your imagination. Now get back to work." (K.
> Klopcic, personal communication, May 24, 2008)

Whether someone is ill, at a distance from a child, in a foreign country fighting a
war, or in any number of other scenarios, humor works.

Chapter 8

More Creative Humor at Work: Professional Settings, Virtual Teams, and Counseling

Humor is useful in all aspects of our personal lives, including whatever we do in our workplaces. Once we internalize the *Humor Perspective*, we can choose when to use humor and be deliberate about doing so. We have briefly discussed the application of the *Humor Perspective* and examples of utility in hospitals and in this chapter, three additional occupational situations are explored: corporate offices, virtual teams, and in counseling. In each environment humor can be utilized to help us lighten up and to help provide enlightenment to others.

The topic of humor in the workplace is the focus for many humorists who do seminars and workshops. An environment that promotes appropriate lightheartedness in approaches to work helps workers cope with pressure and stress (Baum, 2006; Craft & Craft, 1997; Shepell, 2006). Such a workplace fosters creativity and motivation to produce.

The physical surroundings in which we work are important to many of us, so we try to set up an atmosphere that works best for us, physically and aesthetically. Within this environment, many of us interject things that make us smile. Posters, cartoons, and funny quotes to make our personal work environment more pleasant help us feel less stressed but it may be more difficult to spread that lightness throughout the office. Creating a work environment where humor is an integral part takes thoughtful consideration. Is humor acceptable? If so, what types? You are part of a culture that has rules for behavior and that includes both what types of humor are acceptable and when to use it. For example, telling jokes or making funny comments when you feel uncomfortable can backfire and you might be seen as less professional (Toupin, 2006). Humor that is not "politically correct" is not acceptable which means it should not be sexist, profane, racial or ethnic, religious, disparaging of someone else or harassing (Gilbert, 2006). Granirer (2006) agrees and has proposed four "safe humor rules":

- "Don't make jokes about coworkers' sexuality.
- Don't make jokes about people's appearance.
- Avoid jokes about religion, ethnic background, nationality, sexual orientation, and so on, unless it's to joke about your own. If you do not know the rules, it is safest to begin with yourself.
- Avoid jokes about bodily functions. The only exception is if you work in a healthcare or other setting where these jokes are necessary to maintain your sanity (Granirer, 2006, p. 2).

He adds three "safe areas":

- Yourself, your flaws, neuroses, and inadequacies. A self-deprecating comment about something you did may not make anyone laugh but serves to demonstrate you are human, can acknowledge and recover from mistakes and are willing to laugh at yourself. People can relate to these.
- The situation you all face, such as the upcoming merger, the new reorganization, the difficult customers.
- Personal characteristics in areas of low ego-involvement when comments are designed to communicate affection (and acceptance) rather than distain (Granirer, 2006, p. 2).

Even with these guidelines, humor should not be overdone. Gilbert (2006) acknowledges each of us has our own sense of what is funny and at some point there is a chance our humor may offend someone so it is important to know when to keep quiet.

Granirer (2006) defines healthy workplace humor as "acts involving some sort of surprise and/or exaggeration that makes people feel good" (p. 1). He explains that healthy humor for the workplace creates the benefits we have discussed before: relieving tension, creating a sense of acceptance and cohesion, providing a sense of support and restoring a healthy perspective in a given situation (p. 1). He introduces the notion that workplace humor should have a function, one that brings about one or more of these benefits.

Wade, a team member at Hewlett-Packard, describes a workplace that has changed and so has the type of humor utilized. He observed that 10 years ago, most of those in adjoining cubicles were on the same team and so were going in and out of each other's offices sharing personal stories and information. When the team got together, Wade indicated there were hilarious spoofs about personal details because they shared the intimacy and trust of being part of the same group. Now, although people work in adjoining cubicles, they are mostly on different teams and there are fewer cubicle meetings, thus fewer interactions regarding personal experiences. He said the joking now is more cynical and has to do with poking fun at the corporate structure, which he dubbed as *Dilbertesque*, a reference to the popular cartoon, *Dilbert*. He sees the cynicism as bringing about cohesion that is not a given because everyone is on different teams but noted while there is an affable environment, the people are not as "tight and close" as his team was in years past.

Now that we have some guidelines and understanding some of the benefits of humor in the workplace, let's look at some proven techniques. One technique advocated by Norman Cousins (1984) is to start each staff meeting with everyone describing something positive that happened since the last meeting. While that may not be funny, it starts the meeting off on a positive note. To focus specifically on humor, have everyone tell about something that made them laugh. For this to work there have to be some guidelines; Granirer's safe humor rules will work. Keep in mind that whatever you do should be appropriate to your workplace.

Here are some Humor Kit suggestions to start you out (Fahlman, 2005; Granirer, 2006; Klein, 1989; Sultanoff, 1993):

- Give your co-workers gag gifts and funny cards for special occasions. You can always create a special occasion.
- Collect cartoons and let people know you appreciate them by sending an appreciation or grateful gram with a relevant cartoon attached.
- Start a Laughter Board where everyone can post "funnies."
- Start a humor library where anyone can take a break and laugh. Have everyone contribute.
- Use cartoons and humor in your memos. Share Dilbert cartoons.
- Return to favorite cartoons. One of my favorite Gary Larson cartoons shows a warthog cocktail party. Two female warthogs were talking and as another, obviously male, strutted in. One said to the other, "Don't look now but God's gift to warthogs just walked in!"
- Clip funny articles in the newspaper and post them. A *Seattle Times* article identified a website titled "Overhead in New York" that publishes overheard conversations such as:
  Girl 1: Anarchists are so dumb.
  Girl 2: Yeah, totally.
  Girl 3: I mean, just 'cause you hate the government doesn't mean you have to dress badly. (Toosi, 2006, p. A2)
- Have a meeting to discuss ways to inject more humor in your workplace . . . call it a *motivational meeting*.

Virtual offices are relatively new and personnel on virtual teams are generally not in close proximity to each other, possibly not even in the same country.
A virtual team member works in physical isolation from the other team members
and their meetings are conducted primarily over the telephone or through instant
messaging (IM). It is possible many have never met, although in some cases
there are on-site meetings required or the teleworker is free to go to the actual
physical office to work. In addition, team members might be from other cultures. This can cause difficulties among the members and with management.
Members of a team work on projects, the same as on-site teams do; however,
managers and team members may have to develop additional skills to complete
their tasks in remote workplaces. One virtual team member reported he was able
to focus more completely on his work tasks with no interruptions by co-workers.
For other, more social team members, working alone may be problematic. Since
members are not visible to each other, visual non-verbal communication signals
do not exist and one needs to be attuned to auditory cues or written messages
during interactions. These characteristics of the teams are unique but in spite of
the lack of face-to-face interaction, it is business as usual.

One team member, Janet, works at home for a major technology corporation, part of a team that writes technical manuals. She described the experience
of being a virtual team member as having the elements of a new relationship
with the comparable anxiety. She explained sometimes she can tell a new member is anxious by the hesitancy in the voice on the telephone when responding,
stating an opinion, or by a seeming reluctance to talk evidenced by always having to be invited to speak. We learn about what will make others laugh through
frequent interactions, usually face-to-face. That is not possible in the teleworker
situation, so the characteristics of the people on a virtual team are basically un-
known to each other, at least in the beginning. Janet understands the benefits of
humor and wanted to find ways to use humor to help team members relax. She
said the safest type of humor to use is self-disparaging humor. She makes fun of
herself. In the middle of a serious discussion, she might say something like,
"When I can't remember something like that, I make it up." Or she may interject
a comment like, "Can't you read my lips?" and then laugh. She reported that
when she has made comments like this, team members laugh and have become
more forthcoming with their comments. Her joking remarks serve to break the
tension or break the ice and at the same time, she is revealing her own sense of
humor and the absurd. It is probable that the members have learned to look to
her for her wit. Websites that discuss teleworker issues suggest on-line team
members can use on-line card-sending to inject mirth into the operation of a virtual team. While this can help people make connections, demonstrating humor
through verbal interactions seems to be a stronger way to make the group cohe-
sive.

Humor is useful in most situations and can also be effective in the counseling relationship. Ellis (1973) indicated he based his theory of Rational Emotive
Behavioral Therapy (REBT) on the use of humor to help clients challenge their
self-defeating beliefs. Therapists use the ABCDEF process: A for activating

event, B for belief, C for consequences of the behavior, D for disputing the irrational belief (B) with clients to the effect (E) of creating less debilitating beliefs and more productive and positive behaviors. New feelings (F) follow as a result. Ellis believed clients erroneously believe A causes C when, in fact, B causes C and humor can be effective to challenge the irrational belief (B).

When a therapist identifies the irrational belief, for example, "Everyone must love and adore me," a possible response might be, "You must be totally exhausted having to please everyone all of the time. You should go right home and to bed since while you are awake you are constantly pleasing others so they will love and adore you." Or "Is there anyone you have not pleased lately? What happened?" This is followed by something like, "Realistically if everyone does not adore us, it is not the end of the world. We may not like it but we will live." Ellis uses humor to force the client to face an absurd belief that is impacting behavior in a detrimental way.

Many of the benefits of laughter and humor can be created in a counseling relationship. Using humor in the counseling process can help bring about change; however, it should be used carefully and with sensitivity to the client's problem, reaction, and sense of humor. Humorous responses should be spontaneous and well timed (i.e., whether this is an appropriate time to say this). Driscoll (1987) observed that "humor arises spontaneously from the dynamics of the moment and can be easily forgotten by the end of the session." (p. 132). Killinger (1987) noted that as counselors we can model using humor by using it on ourselves first to confront our "conceits and lower our own defenses" and through example "teach a philosophy of humor" to our clients encouraging them to laugh at themselves and be more spontaneous and flexible (p. 38). We have to remember our use of humor must be deliberate and for the client's benefit, not our own.

Killinger (1987) identifies some characteristics of counselors that are necessary in order to effectively use humor in counseling for the benefit of the client. Helpers must have a maturity which includes a wide range of life experiences, the ability to laugh at themselves and their limitations and self-acceptance. She explains that early in the therapeutic relationship the client is working with trust issues and would have to interpret any humorous remarks in the light of whether the counselor is being genuine and trustworthy. Also, in these early stages, the client's sense of humor may not be evident. As trust develops, humor can be introduced gradually and appropriately.

On the other hand, Greenwald (1987) believes the world is an absurd place and he can enjoy the absurdity by using humor. He believes freedom and openness are generated within a humor context and indicated he uses an "informal, humorous" style. He describes his attitude of entering a session deliberately seeking something humorous either in the relationship between him and the client or within the situation the client is facing. He also said he tells stories if they illustrate a point.

In a paper titled "The Use of Humor in Psychoanalysis," Nancy Ronne (1998) reflects:

> One of my foundational assumptions (my bias) is that the use of humor demonstrates a high level of functioning. It adds to life and one's experiences. I am also aware that the use of humor (by both patient and analyst) can be a tool that is used to reduce the intensity and discomfort of painful, horrific or shameful affects. This, also can potentially be destructive to the therapeutic process. (p. 2)

After reviewing pros and cons from reviewing the literature, Ronne concludes that "the choice to use or not to use humor comes from a thoughtful place, not an unconscious enactment" (p. 13). Also, an excessive use of humor by a counselor or therapist can be detrimental, hurtful or, at the very least, not helpful. Frequently, it is used to avoid delicate issues that need to be faced.

Clients who persist in joking and laughing demonstrate an inability to face the threat of what they think they might hear or are unwilling or unable to face personal issues. If the professional with whom they work is also making light of the necessary message, there can be no progress. In addition, confidence and trust in the professional will be eroded. A flip side of the excessive use of humor is when the communicators avoid using certain words in an interaction. This could become funny if the behavior is confronted. Several years ago, I was supervising a marriage counseling session and throughout the session, the couple and the counselor kept referring to "it." When the student walked into the feedback session after the clients had left, I asked, "What was 'it'?" The student said, "Oh, sex." If the partners and the counselor were unwilling to say the word, I question how much value the session had and I wonder where the session might have gone if the word "sex" had been used. What would have happened if the counselor had said, "Is it okay for me to use the 'S' word?" or a similar comedic relief response that would acknowledge what was occurring in the here and now.

There are some critical elements that must be present in order to use humor in counseling. These are not unlike cues to which we attend when we use humor in social situations, but they must be interpreted from a counseling perspective to see if the use of humor will help the client or move the session forward. First, the counselor must have established a relationship characterized by trust and rapport, be sensitive to the client's state of mind and understand where the relationship is in the counseling process. Then, the counselor needs to learn to recognize cues and develop a sensitivity to the client's sense of the world and style of humor. Some relevant cues can be:

- When does the client laugh and at what?
- What types of subjects elicit laughter?
- Is the laughter genuine or does it sound forced or uncomfortable?
- Are the eyes involved? For example, are they part of the laughter or are they exhibiting another emotion? Are they twinkling, teary, hard or flat?
- What is the tone of the client's voice when articulating the humor?

- What does the client's posture tell you?
- What kind of humor is used in the client's world?
- What is the trust level between you and the client?
- Will use of humor move the session forward or distract? Will it be interpreted as intended?
- What is the purpose for using humor? How does culture enter into the use of humor?
- Is this an appropriate time for humor? Will it interfere with what the client is sensing/feeling and be a defense mechanism? Is it relevant?

These are many of the same things we note while counseling, except now we associate what we see and hear with whether the individual is ready for humor. Part of the sensitivity when utilizing humor is recognizing the cues that will lead to when to be funny and when to not be funny, a matter of timing. Also, as in other settings, what is funny to one client may not be to another even though the situation is similar. The most important issue is that the humor used in a counseling session must be used to help and for the benefit of the client, not the counselor.

If we are good observers, we can see evidence of the client's world during the counseling session. Doug Gross, retired counselor educator, provided a good example where he gained some insight from the client's experience even though it was not evident initially:

> In one of my first practicum situations (as a student in training), I was working with a client who complained that the world was against him, and that things just happened to him. I was trying to point out his part in this situation when one of the ceiling tiles in the room I was using fell and hit him in the head. I guess he made his point. (D. Gross, personal communication, July 2006)

Another example where the counselor received some outside help, Brian, a former military counselor, described his first day of unsupervised clinical work:

> My primary patient was K.T., a long-term patient in a short-term, acute care inpatient ward. The average length of stay was 3–7 days and K.T. had been a patient for well over five months at that point. Her diagnosis was MPD (Multiple Personality Disorder), and she was a non-violent, high functioning patient, making her an ideal subject for new staff and the constant stream of students that flowed through this particular teaching hospital. As such, she had, to coin a phrase, "seen it all." She'd been verbally poked and prodded by every nurse, psychology technician, and intern they could throw at her and was more than likely more proficient in the clinical interview than any of them at this point.
>
> Sitting down with her for the first of several planned interactions during the day, I approached the interaction with all the self-serious clinical skill I could muster, maintaining a neutral affect, expressing empathy (say the mantra with

me: but NOT sympathy!!), and the clinical detachment we had been taught to maintain. Needless to say, as I ran through the laundry list of assessment questions she had been asked hundreds of times, her responses were perfunctory at best, utterly bored and mechanical at worst.

While I was running through this exercise, I was aware of another patient, J.K., an extremely high-functioning schizophrenic, who was pacing back and forth nearby, clearly listening to the interaction. As I began to wrap up my by-the-book interaction, since it was apparent that the rapport we'd been taught to expect wasn't developing, I concluded with my question, "Are you having any suicidal ideations?" As I opened my mouth to add this to my string of similar questions, J.K. leaned over between us, stared K.T. in the eye, and asked, "Do you prefer sheep to men?" K.T. burst out laughing, slapping J.K. on the arm and admonishing him; I was unable to contain my own amusement, laughing uncontrollably, despite my intention to remain professional. After this, with my professional shell cracked beyond repair, K.T. and I went on to build a true rapport based not only on the patient-provider relationship, but also on humor and a mutual respect for each other's essential humanity and personalities which, in that moment of admittedly inappropriate humor, had been exposed in the unlikely setting of a locked inpatient psych unit. (B. Freeman, personal communication, (July, 20, 2006).

Becki, a counselor, has

a cartoon file and recommend it to all my clients. On blue or down days, the best "pick me up" is to browse through that file and laugh again at those things that are still as funny as they were the first time you saw them. (R. Brickwedde, personal communication, May 25, 2006)

When used appropriately, humor is a valuable counseling tool to enhance the counseling process. Its use can build rapport, reduce stress and shape new perspectives. Vereen, Butler, Williams, Darg, and Downing (2006) emphasize the need to use humor that is appropriate from a cultural perspective. They specifically discuss the intentional use of humor in the African American culture where "religion is perhaps, the only social construct held in greater esteem than humor, because laughter has served as a means of coping with a challenged past, present and future" (p. 11). Literature supports the effectiveness of using humor in therapy (Maples et al., 2001; Yonkovitz & Matthews, 1998), loosening up defenses (Sloshberg, 1996; Yonkovitz & Matthews, 1998), breaking up stereotypes (Maples et al., 2001), and permitting the expression of hostility and frustration (Yonkovitz & Matthews, 1998). Maples et al. (2001) investigated the cultural perspective and observed that humor is "important in bringing people together and reaffirming bonds of kinship" (pp. 54–55). A caution in counseling anyone from another culture is that your humor must be perceived as relevant and not treating that person's concerns as unimportant. If you are not clear about what you client thinks of as funny, any attempts at using humor might be hurtful.

Chapter 9

Conclusions—Learning to Live the *Humor Perspective*

In a world that is becoming more and more hostile and frightening, seeking the absurdity in our daily lives can be critical to our mental and, in some cases, our physical health. To do this is to adopt the *Humor Perspective*, which means we may have to change some of our attitudes or behaviors. In doing that, each of us will learn more about what makes us chuckle, at the same time acknowledging that there is no universal agreement about what is funny. This seems like a worthwhile endeavor since there is substantial agreement about how laughter and positive attitudes impact our lives as we work and play. The bottom line is that we each have to decide for ourselves what tickles us and learn to be alert for opportunities to laugh, especially at ourselves.

Living the *Humor Perspective* takes time and deliberate effort. We do not necessarily have to *be* funny, just be able to expect something to be humorous and then appreciate it. Lee S. Berk and colleagues (in Oppegaard, 2006) believe anticipation is an important aspect and concluded "significant mood changes can occur even when just thinking about something funny or something about to be funny" (p. D1). Berk stated, "Not only is there real science and psychophysiology, but just the anticipation of the 'mirthful laughter' involved in watching your favorite funny movie has some very surprising and significant neuroendocrine/hormone effects" (Oppegaard, 2006, p.D.1). If this is true, and there is no reason to believe it is not, learning to look for humor in a situation, adopting a *Humor Perspective*, provides us with a unique way to separate or distance ourselves from possible stress. As noted earlier, when we do this and then refocus on the situation, the problem will seem to have changed when in reality our perception is the component that has changed.

If we store what makes us laugh in our mental Humor Kit, later when we remember that story, we can appreciate it all over again. Whether we laugh or perhaps snort, we can have a positive impact on those around us. Just keep in mind, the *Humor Perspective* is about you and can be helpful to you. Corollary benefits, such as entertaining others, are not necessarily the goal of this perspective, though if you are noted for being funny, people will expect to laugh at much of what you say.

We can all profit from seeking absurdities in the world. The intriguing part is that the more we look, the more we find. Theorists, researchers and humorists can explain the intricacies of humor and its scientific benefits, but most of us have already experienced these rewards. Most people will agree genuine laughter feels good and lightens us up, even if only temporarily. Berk and his colleagues (in Oppegaard, 2006) believe this occurs because laughter "triggers the entire limbic system" (p. D7) and physical changes take place. Sultanoff (in Oppegaard, 2006) agrees and emphasizes joy and pain cannot be felt simultaneously.

Beliefs and attitudes formed by experiences within our cultures impact our reactions and can create barriers to using humor. Also, we all encounter circumstances that we do not think are funny and/or where mirth is not appropriate. If we want to incorporate more enjoyment about the incongruities of life, we need to see if any of our personal obstacles are unrealistic and change them. If we look at Wade's earlier comparison of his workplace of today with that of ten years ago (see Chapter 8), he has recognized the trust and intimacy is not the same and the type of humor used ten years ago, teasing about personal information, is not appropriate so the humor is turned outward to focus on the corporation. This is an instance where a realistic barrier is recognized and not violated. He is still laughing about some of the stories that were told ten years ago.

Laughter is useful in many situations if it is used with sensitivity to others involved and to the prevailing climate. Also, remember men and women often appreciate different styles of humor. While jokes may be funny to some, they may not to others. Self-deprecating humor is considered by many to be the safest type of humor to use in groups, however, overuse of this style is inappropriate and is not encouraged as it tends to keep the focus on a single person. Also, it becomes ineffective after awhile. Keep any of your funny comments in your Humor Kit and bring them out at appropriate times. This is where it is also important to understand the reason for injecting humor.

Your mental Humor Kit should contain stories and materials that make you laugh so you can think of them when you need distraction. Many of us do not remember jokes, or at least the punch lines of jokes, but we do remember examples of laughing at ourselves or stories we have heard from others who similarly laughed at themselves. These stories are often more absurd than any joke! The wonderful thing about these stories is years later we still laugh. If you want something more tangible for your kit, Klein (1989) suggests we make a list of all of the curses we would like to be able to use. Number them. Whenever something upsets you, yell one or two of the numbers.

There is a wealth of information about various forms of humor on the Internet. Downloading songs, stories, anecdotes, puns, metaphors, or magic tricks can brighten a day. For the more creative, we can generate our own with some practice. If we do this, what makes us laugh can be fitted to our own experiences. Hence, using a phrase "ring around the collar" can be modified to "wring around the caller" and placed by a telephone if these interruptions cause frustration. If we chuckle before we answer the phone, our voice will sound different than it would if we were irritated at the interruption. Somehow the ensuing conversation is more cordial.

Humor can be introduced into most settings and can create positive results. The keys to remember are:

- Be sensitive
- Be appropriate
- Be alert to cues

Remember, it is bad for your health if you keep your laughter inside. It goes down and spreads to your hips! (Adapted from Fred Allen)

Appendix A

An Unfinished List of Ways to Add Humor and Play to Your Life

The ways we can laugh are limited only by our own inability to create new ways to make ourselves laugh without hurting anyone. This chapter identifies some that have been successful. Add your own. In addition, there are some contributions from personal emails that I could not resist including. Those that tickle your funnybone can be spread around. Collect cartoons, funny articles, humorous incidents, stories etc.

- Go to the zoo—make the monkeys laugh. While at the zoo, spend some time watching and talking to the apes.
- Go on a metaphor hunt.
- Learn to juggle—try scarves first then graduate to whatever you can lift!
- Buy a joke-a-day calendar and share each one. It does not matter if you read it to the other person or you tell it—share it with someone.
- Get on the elevator, face the back or face the front and sing.
- Learn magic tricks and teach it to someone else. Go to a magic shop and shop!
- Take a humor package to a shut-in friend (I've used *Calvin & Hobbes*, the *Far Side* cartoons and *The Journal of Irreproducible Results*).
- Invite a grouch to lunch. Wear a "Take a Grouch to Lunch" button or one that says "National Grouch Week . . . I am a role model" or both.
- When your money comes out of the ATM, scream "I won!", "I won!!" "Third time this week!!!!" (T. Lytle, personal communication, September 12, 2005)
- Page yourself over the intercom. Don't disguise your voice." (T. Lytle, personal communication, September 12, 2005)

- Play with young children.
- Go to a toy store and play with the toys.
- Play "Calvin Ball" where you make up the rules as you go along
- Ask people to tell you a personal funny story or anything they have observed that was funny. Join in their laughter.
- Take fifteen minutes to watch the clouds go by. See if any are in a familiar shape.
- Unplug your television set for twenty-fours or longer.
- Get up on the other side of the bed. Do not apologize if you have to crawl over someone. Conversely, get into bed on the other side of the bed.
- Go to bed with your shoes on.
- Read Hugh Prather's *Spiritual Games*.
- Call a meeting. Burn the agenda.
- Spend some time in the humor section of a bookstore.
- Take a puppy to a senior citizen's center.
- Buy something outrageous.
- Wear a Halloween costume. Do not worry if it is not Halloween.
- Make a mistake and practice laughing at yourself when you do. I met an elderly man who told me unless he made at least one mistake a day and laughed at it, it was not a good day.
- Do something uncharacteristic of you and enjoy your reaction.
- Develop and distribute "Humor Coupons," for example, "Turn in for a genuine laugh," "Thank you for making me laugh," or "Thank you for making my day brighter."
- Make up a list of adages and complete them yourself, for example, "Don't count your chickens . . . " (until they are all in the coop or soup), "Don't look a gift horse . . . " (from the wrong end), "Love all, trust . . . "(maybe your mother), "A penny saved is . . . " (worthless). Place your new adages in prominent places.
- Look around you for humor. Practice the *Humor Perspective*.
- Learn to laugh at yourself.
- Have a Whine and Cheese party. Exaggerate your trials and tribulations. Send invitations. Have partygoers focus on something that has happened recently they consider negative. Have them whine to each other about the incident, exaggerating until they begin to laugh. Once everyone has practiced this, say Cheese (that is what photographers do to get people to smile). Then have everyone at your party focus on positive things that have happened to them during the previous few days.
- Practice giving yourself a standing ovation in your head or patting yourself on the back. Learn to appreciate yourself and not wait for someone else to acknowledge you.

- Watch old episodes of television programs from the days of Mary Tyler Moore, Lucille Ball, Jack Benny, Red Skeleton, Victor Borge, Bob Hope, and many more. I found *Chuckles Bites the Dust* with Mary Tyler Moore at Amazon.com.
- Create puns, metaphors or caricatures about things that are frustrating to you.
- Blow bubbles.
- Klein (1989) suggests that we keep a running list that names all of the people who angered us during the week on toilet paper. At the end of that week, we can flush it.

Internet contributions forwarded by friends:

- Visit the Pike Place Market Fish Market in Seattle and watch the workers toss fish.
- Read the comics page of a newspaper.
- Volunteer to be Santa Claus or the Easter Bunny.

Jeanne Segal suggests the following (Segal, 2006):

- Take an improvisation comedy class.
- Throw a costume party.
- Make faces in the mirror when alone.
- Practice playing. Play with animals, babies and young children, and customer service people.

Appendix B

Just for Laughs

There is a rule of the thumb that for good health, we need 15 belly laughs a day. Most of us are running on a deficit! Put one of these sayings where you can see and share them . . . the water cooler, refrigerator, bathroom mirror????

Quotes by Great Ladies
(contributed by J. Dode, personal communication, May 12, 2006)

Inside every older lady is a younger lady—wondering what the hell happened.
– Cora Harvey Armstrong –

Inside me lives a skinny woman crying to get out. But I can usually shut her up with cookies.
– Tracy Briseno –

The hardest years in life are those between ten and seventy.
– Helen Hayes (at 73) –

I refuse to think of them as chin hairs. I think of them as stray eyebrows.
– Janette Barber –

Things are going to get a lot worse before they get worse.
– Lily Tomlin –

A male gynecologist is like an auto mechanic who never owned a car.
– Carrie Snow –

Laugh and the world laughs with you. Cry and you cry with your girlfriends.
– Laurie Kuslansky –

My second favorite household chore is ironing. My first being, hitting my head on the top bunk bed until I faint.
– Erma Bombeck –

Old age ain't no place for sissies.
– Bette Davis –

A man's got to do what a man's got to do. A woman must do what he can't.
– Rhonda Hansome –

The phrase "working mother" is redundant.
– Jane Sellman –

Every time I close the door on reality, it comes in through the windows.
– Jennifer Unlimited –

Whatever women must do they must do twice as well as men to be thought half as good. Luckily, this is not difficult.
– Charlotte Whitton –

Thirty-five is when you finally get your head together and your body starts falling apart.
– Caryn Leschen –

I try to take one day at a time—but sometimes several days attack me at once.
– Jennifer Unlimited –

If you can't be a good example—then you'll just have to be a horrible warning.
– Catherine –

When I was young, I was put in a school for retarded kids for two years before they realized I actually had a hearing loss. And they called ME slow!
– Kathy Buckley –

I'm not offended by all the dumb blonde jokes because I know 'm not dumb -- and I'm also not blonde.
– Dolly Parton –

If high heels were so wonderful, men would still be wearing them.
– Sue Grafton –

I'm not going to vacuum 'til Sears makes one you can ride on.
– Roseanne Barr –

When women are depressed they either eat or go shopping. Men invade another country.
– Elayne Boosler –

In politics, if you want anything said, ask a man. If you want anything done, ask a woman.
– Margaret Thatcher –

I have yet to hear a man ask for advice on how to combine marriage and a career.
– Gloria Steinem –

I am a marvelous housekeeper. Every time I leave a man, I keep his house.
– Zsa Zsa Gabor –

Nobody can make you feel inferior without your permission.
– Eleanor Roosevelt –

One thing that seems to bother many people is the fact that they are aging. Think about conversations you have had when someone mentioned a physical complaint and the response was, "Well that's part of the aging process" or "It's rough getting old." While it is true we are aging from the moment we are born, and yes, as we get older the body makes itself heard, but everyone already knows this. Does this really need repeating? The following are ideas others have about coping with aging. Both have been widely published on the internet. The first one is often credited to George Carlin and the second to Julie Andrews, and the authenticity of the both sources has been questioned. Nevertheless, they have a unique perspective on aging:

George Carlin's View on Aging
(contributed by G. Schultz, personal communication, May 1, 2006)

Do you realize that the only time in our lives when we like to get old is when we're kids? If you're less than 10 years old, you're so excited about aging that you think in fractions.

"How old are you?" "I'm four and a half!" You're never thirty-six and a half. You're four and a half, going on five! That's the key.

You get into your teens, now they can't hold you back. You jump to the next number, or even a few ahead.

"How old are you?" "I'm gonna be 16!" You could be 13, but hey, you're gonna be 16! And then the greatest day of your life . . . You become 21. Even the words sound like a ceremony . . . YOU BECOME 21. YESSSS!!!

But then you turn 30. Oooohh, what happened there? Makes you sound like bad milk! He TURNED; we had to throw him out. There's no fun now, you're just a sour-dumpling. What's wrong? What's changed?

You BECOME 21, you TURN 30, then you're PUSHING 40. Whoa! Put on the brakes, it's all slipping away. Before you know it, you REACH 50.

And your dreams are gone.

But wait!!! You MAKE it to 60. You didn't think you would!

So you BECOME 21, TURN 30, PUSH 40, REACH 50 and MAKE it to   60.

You've built up so much speed that you HIT 70! After that it's a day-by-day thing; you HIT Wednesday!

You get into your 80s and every day is a complete cycle; you HIT lunch; you TURN 4:30; you REACH bedtime. And it doesn't end there. Into the 90s, you start going backwards; "I Was JUST 92."

Then a strange thing happens. If you make it over 100, you become a little kid again. "I'm 100 and a half!"

May you all make it to a healthy 100 and a half!!

Here is a song about aging to be sung to the tune of My Favorite Things from the Sound of Music (contributed by I. Dode, personal communication, May 4, 2006):

Maalox and nose drops and needles for knitting,
Walkers and handrails and new dental fittings,
Bundles of magazines tied up in string,
These are a few of my favorite things.

Cadillacs and cataracts and hearing aids and glasses,
Polident and Fixodent and false teeth in glasses,
Pacemakers, golf carts and porches with swings,
These are a few of my favorite things.

When the pipes leak,
When the bones creak,
When the knees go bad,
I simply remember my favorite things,
And then I don't feel so bad.

Hot tea and crumpets and corn pads for bunions,
No spicy hot food or food cooked with onions,
Bathrobes and heating pads and hot meals they bring,
These are a few of my favorite things.

Back pains, confused brains, and no fear of sinnin',
Thin bones and fractures and hair that is thinnin',
And we won't mention our short shrunken frames,
When we remember our favorite things.

When the joints ache,
When the hips break,
When the eyes grow dim,
Then I remember the great life I've had,
And then I don't feel so bad.

Growing older is difficult for some people and someone coined the following advice:

How to Stay Young

1. Throw out nonessential numbers. This includes age, weight and height. Let the doctors worry about them. That is why you pay them.

2. Keep only cheerful friends. The grouches pull you down. (Keep this in mind if you are one of those grouches.)

3. Enjoy the simple things.

4. Laugh often, long and loud. Laugh until you gasp for breath. And if you have a friend who makes you laugh, spend lots and lots of time with HIM/HER.

5. The tears happen: Endure, grieve, and move on. The only person who is with you your entire life, is you. LIVE while you are alive."

(G. Schultz, personal communication, July 19, 2006)

Since growing older is developmental, so is what we learn along the way. At each stage we learn different "wisdoms":

Great Truths about Life that Little Children Have Learned

- No matter how hard you try, you can't baptize cats.
- When your Mom is mad at your Dad, don't let her brush your hair.
- If your sister hits you, don't hit her back. They always catch the second person.
- Never ask your 3-year-old brother to hold a tomato.
- Reading what people write on desks can teach you a lot.
- School lunches stick to the wall.
- You can't hide a piece of broccoli in a glass of milk.
- Don't wear polka-dot underwear under white shorts.

Great Truths about Life that Adults Have Learned

- There is always a lot to be thankful for, if you take the time to look. For example, I'm sitting here thinking how nice it is that wrinkles don't hurt.
- The best way to keep kids at home is to make a pleasant atmosphere—and let the air out of their tires.
- Today's mighty oak is just yesterday's nut that held its ground.
- Laughing helps. It's like jogging on the inside.
- Middle age is when you choose your cereal for the fiber, not the toy.
- My mind not only wanders; sometimes it leaves completely.
- If you can remain calm, you just don't have all the facts.

Great Truths about Growing Old

- Growing old is mandatory; growing up is optional.
- Forget the health food. I need all the preservatives I can get.
- You know you're getting old when you stoop and tie your shoes and wonder what else you can do while you're down there.

- It's frustrating when you know all the answers, but nobody bothers to ask you the questions.
- Time may be a great healer, but it's also a lousy beautician.
- Amazing! You just hang something in your closet for a while, and it shrinks two sizes.
- Inside of us is a thin person struggling to get out, but they can usually be sedated with a few pieces of chocolate cake."

(G. Schultz, personal communication, February 10, 2006)

Another way to stay young is to spend time around children:

A little boy was in a relative's wedding. As he was coming down the aisle, he would take two steps, stop, and turn to the crowd. While facing the crowd, he would put his hands up like claws and roar. So it went, step, step, ROAR, step, step, ROAR, all the way down the aisle. As you can imagine, the crowd was near tears from laughing so hard by the time he reached the pulpit. When asked what he was doing, the child sniffed and said, "I was being the Ring Bear."

One Sunday in a Midwest City, a young child was "acting up" during the morning worship hour. The parents did their best to maintain some sense of order in the pew but were losing the battle. Finally, the father picked the little fellow up and walked sternly up the aisle on his way out. Just before reaching the safety of the foyer, the little one called loudly to the congregation, "Pray for me! Pray for me!"

One particular four-year-old prayed, "And forgive us our trash baskets as we forgive those who put trash in our baskets."

A little boy was overheard praying: "Lord, if you can't make me a better boy, don't worry about it. I'm having a real good time like I am."

A Sunday school teacher asked her little children, as they were on the way to church service, "And why is it necessary to be quiet in church?"
One bright little girl replied, "Because people are sleeping."

A little boy opened the big and old family Bible with fascination, looking at the old pages as he turned them. Then something fell out of the Bible. He picked it up and looked at it closely. It was an old leaf from a tree that has been pressed in between the pages. "Mama, look what I found," the boy called out. "What have you got there, dear?" his mother asked. With astonishment in the young boy's voice he answered, "It's Adam's suit."

~~~~~

The preacher was wired for sound with a lapel mike, and as he preached, he moved briskly about the platform, jerking the mike cord as he went. Then he moved to one side, getting wound up in the cord and nearly tripping before jerking it again. After several circles and jerks, a little girl in the third pew leaned toward her mother and whispered, "If he gets loose, will he hurt us?"

~~~~~

Six-year old Angie, and her four-year old brother, Joel, were sitting together in church. Joel giggled, sang and talked out loud. Finally, his big sister had had enough. "You're not supposed to talk out loud in church." "Why? Who's going to stop me?" Joel asked. Angie pointed to the back of the church and said, "See those two men standing by the door? They're hushers."

~~~~~

A ten-year-old, under the tutelage of her grandmother, was becoming quite knowledgeable about the Bible. Then, one day, she floored her grandmother by asking, "Which Virgin was the mother of Jesus? The virgin Mary or the King James Virgin?"

~~~~~

A Sunday school class was studying the Ten Commandments. They were ready to discuss the last one. The teacher asked if anyone could tell her what it was. Susie raised her hand, stood tall, and quoted, "Thou shall not take covers off the neighbor's wife."

(D. Paul, personal communication, February 21, 2006)

Children have the ability to create humor in the most innocent manner. As adults it seems many of us censor what we say. Children often have another perspective and are more spontaneous. Here are some personal stories:

My brother, Ed, asked his son, Gavin, how long he figured it would take him to complete first grade. Gavin replied smugly, "Papa, first grade only takes one year . . . but second grade takes two years." His dad said, "Wait a minute. At that rate I'll be retired before you get out of grade school." Gavin replied, "No you won't—you'll be dead!"

~~~~~

My niece, Amanda, who had just had braces placed on her teeth told me, "You know Aunt Sandra, I think I want to be an orthodontist when I grow up." I acknowledged her choice, and noted she could be whatever she wanted to be. She asked me how long she might have to go to school to be an orthodontist. I explained about finishing a four-year degree, completing a dental degree, and studying for a specialization. She listened carefully and said, "Wow, by then you will be taking three naps a day!" Of course, all present burst out laughing and she was so proud to have made us all laugh so hard!

~~~~~

My nephew, Michael, eight years old, had damaged a new kitchen knife. When my twin brother asked who did it, none of the three children would confess. So, using Dreikurs and Soltz's (1964) Children the Challenge rules to interact with children, my brother told the three that no one would be able to do anything after school until someone confessed. Both girls came to him and told him Michael had done the deed. His response was always, "I need to hear that from Michael." After a day or so, he returned to his office from lunch, and his office associate told him he had had the strangest telephone call. He explained a child had called and said, "I confess. I did it." and hung up! Apparently Michael's sisters had put on some pressure.

Additional selected email contributions I could not resist:

Actual Newspaper Ads

FREE YORKSHIRE TERRIER: 8 years old. Hateful little mutt. Bites.

FREE PUPPIES: 1/2 Cocker Spaniel, 1/2 sneaky neighbor's dog.

FREE PUPPIES: Part German Shepherd, part stupid dog.

FREE GERMAN SHEPHERD: 85 lbs. Neutered. Speaks German.

FOUND DIRTY WHITE DOG: Looks like a rat. . . . Been out a while. Better be a reward for this nasty little thing.

COWS, CALVES: NEVER BRED. Also 1 gay bull for sale.

NORDIC TRACK $300: Hardly used, call Chubby.

GEORGIA PEACHES: California grown—89 cents lb.

JOINING NUDIST COLONY! Must sell washer and dryer
$300.

WEDDING DRESS FOR SALE. WORN ONCE BY MISTAKE: Call
Stephanie.

(C. Renfrew-Starry, personal communication, February 10, 2006)

Another gem from the Internet contains real responses to airplane repair reports.
These are excellent examples of using the *Humor Perspective* on the job:

Pilot (P): Left inside main tire almost needs replacement.
Mechanic Supervisor (S): Almost replaced left inside main tire.

P: Test flight OK, except auto-land very rough.
S: Auto-land not installed on this aircraft.

P: Something loose in cockpit.
S: Something tightened in cockpit.

P: Dead bugs on windshield.
S: Live bugs on back-order.

P: Autopilot in altitude-hold mode produces a 200 feet per minute descent.
S: Cannot reproduce problem on ground.

P: Evidence of leak on right main landing gear.
S: Evidence removed.

P: DME volume unbelievably loud.
S: DME volume set to more believable level.

P: Friction locks cause throttle levers to stick.
S: That's what they're for.

P: IFF inoperative.

S: IFF always inoperative in OFF mode.

P: Suspected crack in windshield.
S: Suspect you're right.

P: Number 3 engine missing.
S: Engine found on right wing after brief search.

P: Aircraft handles funny.
S: Aircraft warned to straighten up, fly right, and be serious.

P: Target radar hums.
S: Reprogrammed target radar with lyrics.

P: Mouse in cockpit.
S: Cat installed.

P: Noise coming from under instrument panel. Sounds like a midget pounding on something with a hammer.
S: Took hammer away from midget.

An airline pilot wrote that on this particular flight he had hammered his ship into the runway really hard. The airline had a policy which required the first officer to stand at the door while the passengers exited, smile, and give them a "Thanks for flying our airline." He said that, in light of his bad landing, he had a hard time looking the passengers in the eye, thinking that someone would have a smart comment. Finally everyone had gotten off except for a little old lady walking with a cane. She said, "Sir, do you mind if I ask you a question?" "Why, no, Ma'am," said the pilot. "What is it?" The little old lady said, "Did we land, or were we shot down?" (contributed by G. Schultz, personal communication, March 1, 2006)

As we progress through life, here are some "Words to Live By":

- Accept that some days you're the pigeon, and some days you're the statue.
- Always read stuff that will make you look good if you die in the middle of it.
- Drive carefully. It's not only cars that can be recalled by their maker.
- Eat a live toad in the morning and nothing worse will happen to you for the rest of the day.
- If you can't be kind, at least have the decency to be vague.

- If you lend someone $20 and never see that person again, it was probably worth it.
- It may be that your sole purpose in life is simply to serve as a warning to others.
- Never buy a car you can't push.
- Never put both feet in your mouth at the same time, because then you don't have a leg to stand on.
- The early worm gets eaten by the bird, so sleep late.
- When everything's coming your way, you're in the wrong lane.
- Birthdays are good for you; the more you have, the longer you live.
- You may be only one person in the world, but you may also be the world to one person.
- Some mistakes are too much fun to only make once.
- Don't cry because it's over, smile because it happened.
- We could learn a lot from crayons: some are sharp, some are pretty, some are dull, some have weird names, and all are different colors but they all have to learn to live in the same box.
- A truly happy person is one who can enjoy the scenery on a detour.
- Happiness comes through doors you didn't even know you left open.

(G. Schultz, personal communication, June 15, 2006)

Some humor is unintentional as found in the following list of headlines:

Actual Newspaper Headlines
(Collected by Actual Journalists)

1. Something Went Wrong in Jet Crash, Expert Says

2. Police Begin Campaign to Run Down Jaywalkers

3. Safety Experts Say School Bus Passengers Should Be Belted

4. Drunk Gets Nine Months in Violin Case

5. Farmer Bill Dies in House

6. Stud Tires Out

7. Soviet Virgin Lands Short of Goal Again

8. British Left Waffles on Falkland Islands

9. Teacher Strikes Idle Kids

10. Reagan Wins on Budget, But More Lies Ahead

11. Squad Helps Dog Bite Victim

12. Shot Off Woman's Leg Helps Nicklaus to 66

13. Enraged Cow Injures Farmer with Ax

14. Plane Too Close to Ground, Crash Probe Told

15. Stolen Painting Found by Tree

16. Two Sisters Reunited after 18 Years in Checkout Counter

17. War Dims Hope for Peace

18. If Strike isn't Settled Quickly, It May Last a While

19. Cold Wave Linked to Temperatures

20. Enfields Couple Slain; Police Suspect Homicide

21. Red Tape Holds Up New Bridge

22. Deer Kill 17,000

23. Man Struck by Lightning Faces Battery Charge

24. New Study of Obesity Looks for Larger Test Group

25. Astronaut Takes Blame for Gas in Spacecraft

26. Lansing Residents Can Drop Off Trees

27. Steals Clock, Faces Time

28. Old School Pillars are replaced by Alumni

(Nilsen & Nilsen, 2006)

One could ponder these questions that really need answers and create great responses:

1. Who was the first person to look at a cow and say, "I think I'll squeeze these dangly things here, and drink whatever comes out?"

2. Who was the first person to say, "See that chicken there? I'm gonna eat the next thing that comes outta its butt."

3. Why is there a light in the fridge and not in the freezer?

4. If Jimmy cracks corn and no one cares, why is there a song about him?

5. Can a hearse carrying a corpse drive in the carpool lane?

6. Why does Goofy stand erect while Pluto remains on all fours? They're both dogs!

7. If quizzes are quizzical, what are tests?

8. If corn oil is made from corn, and vegetable oil is made from vegetables, then what is baby oil made from?

9. If electricity comes from electrons, does morality come from morons?

10. Why do the *Alphabet Song* and *Twinkle, Twinkle Little Star* have the same tune?

11. Do illiterate people get the full effect of Alphabet Soup?

12. Did you ever notice that when you blow in a dog's face, he gets mad at you, but when you take him on a car ride, he sticks his head out the window?

13. Does pushing the elevator button more than once make it arrive faster?

14. Why doesn't glue stick to the inside of the bottle?

(G. Schultz, personal communication, May 4, 2006)

For those of you who are writers, these rules may be helpful . . . or not!

- Verbs HAS to agree with their subjects.
- Prepositions are not words to end sentences with.
- And don't start a sentence with a conjunction.
- It is wrong to ever split an infinitive.
- Be more or less specific.
- Parenthetical remarks (however relevant) are (usually) unnecessary.
- No sentence fragments.
- Also, too, never, ever use repetitive redundancies.
- Contractions aren't necessary and shouldn't be used.
- One word sentences? Eliminate.
- Puns are for children, not groan readers.
- Exaggeration is a billion times worse than understatement.

(G. Schultz, personal communication, March 12, 2006)

For pet owners:

The Dog's Diary

7 am—Oh boy! A walk! My favorite!
8 am—Oh boy! Dog food! My favorite!
9 am—Oh boy! The kids! My favorite!
Noon—Oh boy! The yard! My favorite!
2 pm—Oh boy! A car ride! My favorite!
3 pm—Oh boy! The kids! My favorite!
4 pm—Oh boy! Playing ball! My favorite!
6 pm—Oh boy! Welcome home Mom! My favorite!
7 pm—Oh boy! Welcome home Dad! My favorite!
8 pm—Oh boy! Dog food! My favorite!
9 pm—Oh boy! Tummy rubs on the couch! My favorite!
11 pm—Oh boy! Sleeping in my people's bed! My favorite!

The Cat's Diary

Day 183 of my captivity. . . . My captors continued to taunt me with bizarre little dangling objects. They dine lavishly on fresh meat, while I am forced to eat dry cereal. The only thing that keeps me going is the hope of escape, and the mild satisfaction I get from clawing the furniture.

Tomorrow I may eat another houseplant. Today my attempt to kill my captors by weaving around their feet while they were walking almost succeeded—must try this at the top of the stairs. In an attempt to disgust and repulse these vile oppressors, I once again induced myself to vomit on their favorite chair—must try this on their bed.

Decapitated a mouse and brought them the headless body in an attempt to make them aware of what I am capable of, and to try to strike fear in their hearts. They only cooed and condescended about what a good little cat was! Hmmm, not working according to plan.

There was some sort of gathering of their accomplices. I was placed in solitary throughout the event. However, I could hear the noise and smell the food. More important, I overheard that my confinement was due to my powers of inducing "allergies." Must learn what this is and how to use it to my advantage.

I am convinced the other captives are flunkies and maybe snitches. The dog is routinely released and seems more than happy to return. He is obviously a half-wit. The bird, on the other hand, has got to be an informant and speaks with them regularly. I am certain he reports my every move. Due to his current placement in the metal room, his safety is assured. But I can wait; it is only a matter of time.

(G. Schultz, personal communication, February 25, 2006)

Advice from Maxine, "Don't go to bed angry. Stay up and plot your revenge." (J. Lundquist, personal communication, July 20, 2006)

Appendix C

Resources

Resources for Humor and Play

There are many websites the contain information about humor. Some of these are personal/business websites for humor consultants or humorists who do workshops and seminars on the topic of humor and others contain articles and excerpts from publications related to the subject. Doing an Internet search for humor or laughter will yield a lengthy list of possible resources. Since websites change, I have listed some websites and materials I have used to design the Creative Humor at Work Seminar and some that have been around for many years. You can use a search engine to discover those that will work best for you. Here are just a few that contain information or materials I have enjoyed using:

www.humorproject.com
The Humor Project Inc.
480 Broadway, Suite 210
Saratoga Springs, NY 12866
518.587.8770
Contains products, books, magazines, all designed to elicit laughter, e.g., *Laughing Matters* and *Readers Di-Jest* and current information about humor.

www.playfair.com
Playfair is also the name of a book containing a wealth of non-competitive games for groups of all sizes. This website lists additional resources.

www.worldlaughtertour.com

For Puns:
   www.ocii.com/~cmeek/puns.htm
   www.lyngperry/humor/story01.htm
   www.workinghumor.com
   www.badpuns.com

For information about and examples of metaphors:
   www.knowgramming.com
   www.theliterarylink.com

Books

These books have been invaluable in teaching people about "letting go" of any inhibitions and creating their own humor. While some may be out-of-date, if you go to the website (Google New Games Foundation or www.inewgames) there appear to be copies available and the games do not go out-of-date. There are also additional resources on that website. The Von Oech books are at www.amazon.com.

New Games Foundation (1976). *The new games book* (A. Fluegelman, Ed.). New York: Doubleday & Company.
New Games Foundation (1981). *More new games* (A Fluegelman, Ed.). New York: Doubleday & Company.
Scherr, G. H. (Ed.) (1976). *The journal of irreproducible results*. Chicago Heights, IL: J. I. R. Publishers.
Von Oech, R. (1983). *A whack on the side of the head: How to unlock your mind for innovation*. New York: Warner Books.
Von Oech, R. (1986) *A kick in the seat of the pants*. New York: Harper & Row.

References

Adler, A. (1957) *Understanding human nature*. New York: Premier Books.
Alexander, R. D. (1986). Ostracism and indirect reciprocity: The reproductive significance of humor. *Ethiology and Sociobiology*, 7(3–4), 253–270.
American Heritage Dictionary of the English Language (4th ed.). (2003). Boston: Houghton Mifflin Company.
Barreca, R. (1991). *They used to call me Snow White but I drifted: Women's strategis use of humor*. New York: Viking Penguin.
Barrett, J. (n.d.). When women laugh it's no joke. Retrieved April 5, 2005, from the Internet.
Baum, R. B. (1998). *Humor and disability*. Retrieved April 6, 2006, from State University College at Buffalo Web site: http://www.buffalostate.edu/library

Berk, L., & S. L. Tan. (1999, March 11). Therapeutic benefits of laughter. Loma Linda School of Medicine News. Retrieved September 26, 2006, from http://www.holistic-online.com/Humor _Therapy/

Berk, L., Tan S. A., & Westengard, J. (2006, April). Beta-Endorphin and HGH increase are associated with both the anticipation and experience of mirthful laughter. Paper presented to the APS Behavioral Neuroscience & Drug Abuse Section, San Francisco, CA.

Berk L., & Bittman, B. (1999, March). SMILE (Subjective Multidimensional Interactive Laughter Evaluation). Loma Linda School of Medicine News. Retrieved September 26, 2006, from http://www.llu.ed/news

Bippus, A. M. (2003). Humor motives, qualities, and reactions in recalled conflict episodes. *Western Journal of Communications, 67*. Retrieved May 4, 2006, from http://www.questia.com

Block, S., Browning, S., & McGrath, G. (1983). Humor in group psychology. *British Journal of Medical Psychology. 56*, 89–97.

Boehner, J. (February 13, 2006). Notebook. *Time, 167*(7), 13.

Bressler, E., & Balshine, S. (2006, January). A good sense of humor will get you a date. *Evolution and Human Behavior, 27*, 29–39.

Brooks, J. L. & Burns, A. (1992). *The Mary Tyler Moore show: Chuckles bites the dust*. Studio City, CA: MTM Enterprises.

Campbell, R. (February 7, 2005). What's laughter got to do with it? A sense of humor's important in love, but what does it mean? *The Journal Times*. Retrieved April 26, 2006, from www.journaltimes.com/articles

Chafe, W. (1987). Humor as a disabling mechanism. *American Behavioral Scientist, 30*(1), 16–25.

Coleman, M. (2005, November/December). Is laughter really the best medicine? *Journal on Active Aging*, 77.

Cousins, N. (1979). *Anatomy of an illness as perceived by the patient: Reflections on healing and regeneration*. New York: Bantam Books.

Cousins, N. (1989). *Head first: The biology of hope*. New York: E. P. Dutton

Craft, B., & Craft, K. (1997, May). Humor in the workplace. *Innovative Leader, 6(5)*. Retrieved August 28, 2006 from http://www.winstonbrill.com

Dingfelder, S. F. (2006). The formula for funny. *Monitor on Psychology, 37*(6), 55.

Dreikurs, R., & Soltz, V. (1964). *Children the challenge*. New York: Hawthorn Books.

Driscoll, R. (1987). Humor in pragmatic psychotherapy. In W. F. Fry, Jr., & W. A. Salameh (Eds.), *Handbook of humor and psychotherapy: Advances in the clinical use of humor* (pp. 127–147). Sarasota, FL: Professional Resource Exchange.

Eagly, A.H. & Steffen, V.J. (1986). Gender and helping behavior: A meta-analytic review of the social psychological literature. *Psychological Bulletin, 100*(3), p. 283–308.

Ellis, A. (1973). *Humanistic psychotherapy: The rational-emotive approach.* New York: Julian Press and McGraw-Hill Paperbacks.

Ellis, A. (1977–1985). *A Garland of Rational Songs.* New York, New York: Institute for Rational Emotive Therapy.

Fahlman, C. (2005–6). *Humor at work.* Retrieved April 26, 2006, from http://home.teleport.com/~laff9to5

Ferguson, M., Coleman, W., & Perrin, P. (1990). *Book of the pragmagic.* New York: Simon & Schuster.

Freud, S. (1905/1966). *Jokes and their relation to the unconscious.* London: Routlege & Kegan Paul.

Gascon, D. (2004). *Humor for your health.* Retrieved April 26, 2006 from www.humorforyourhealth.com

Gilbert, F. (2006). *"Your Fired"—Humor in the Workplace.* Retrieved August 28, 2006, from www.originallyspeaking.com/blog/2006/03/your-fired-humor-in-the-workplace/

Gladding, S. (2006). *Use of metaphors in counseling.* Unpublished manuscript.

Gladding, S. (in press). *Becoming a counselor: The light, the bright, and the serious* (2nd ed.). Alexandria, VA: American Counseling Association Foundation.

Glasser, W. (1965). *Reality therapy.* New York: Harper & Row.

Goodman, J. (1984, Fall). Workshop on "Laughter and Creativity" in Seattle, WA.

Granirer, D. (2006). *Welcome to the new reality: Navigating the quagmire of humor and political correctness.* Retrieved August 28, 2006, from www.granirer.com/ART-0001.htm

Greenwald, H. (1987). The humor decision. In W. F. Fry, Jr., & W. A. Salameh (Eds.), *Handbook of humor and psychotherapy: Advances in the clinical use of humor* (pp. 41–54). Sarasota, FL: Professional Resource Exchange.

Haig, R. A. (October, 1986) Therapeutic uses of humor. *American Journal of Psychotherapy, Vol. XL, No. 4.*

Humor and mental health: Using humor to cope with stress. Retrieved, March 29, 2006, from http://www.corexcel.com/html/body.humor.page 8.htm

Joshua, A. M., Cotroneo, A., & Clarke, S. (2005). Art of oncology: When the tumor is not the target. *American Society of Clinical Oncology, 23*(3), 645–648.

Killinger, B. (1987). Humor in psychotherapy: A shift to a new perspective. In W. F. Fry, Jr., & W. A. Salameh (Eds.), *Handbook of humor and psychotherapy: Advances in the clinical use of humor* (pp. 21–40). Sarasota, FL: Professional Resource Exchange.

Klein, A. (1989). *The healing power of humor: Techniques for getting through loss, setbacks, upsets, disappointments, difficulties, trials, tribulations, and all that not-so-funny stuff.* Los Angeles: Jerremy P. Tarcher.

Mahony, D. (2000). Is laughter the best medicine or any medicine at all? *Eye on Psi Chi, 4*(3), 18–21.

Maples, M. F., Dupey, P., Torres-Rivera, E., Phan, L. T., Vereen, L., & Garrett, M. T. (2001). Ethnic diversity and the use of humor in counseling: Appropriate or inappropriate. *Journal of Counseling & Development, 79*, 53–60.

Martin, R. A. (2001). Humor, laughter, and physical health: Methodological issues and research findings. *Psychological Bulletin, 127(4)*, 504–519.

McCahn, J. (n.d.). Serious humor. *Arizona State University Research Magazine.* Retrieved April 25, 2006, from http://researchmag.asu.edu/stories/humor3.html

McGhee, P. (1999). Adapted from *Health, Healing and the Amuse System: Humor as Survival Training.* Retrieved April 26, 2006, from http://www.corexcel.com

McGhee, P. (1979). The role of laughter and humor in growing up female. In C. B. Kopp, (Ed.), *Becoming Female: Perspectives on development* (pp. 183–206). New York: Plenum.

Meeks, C. (2006). *Page of puns.* Retrieved April 25, 2005, from http://www.ocii.com/~cmeek/index.htm

Myers, J. E., Sweeney, T. J., & Witmer, J. M. (2000). The wheel of wellness counseling for wellness: A holistic model for treatment planning. *Journal of Counseling & Development, 78(3)*, 251–266.

New Orleans hurricane humor searching for gales of laughter. (2006, February 28). *The Seattle Times*, p. A14.

Nilsen, A., & Nilsen, D. L. F. (2000). *Encyclopedia of 20th century of American humor.* Phoenix, AZ: Oryx Press.

Oldenburg, D. (2005, May 1). Laugh yourself skinny. *The Seattle Times*, p. K4.

Oppegaard, B. (2006, September 17). Anatomy of a laugh: Amusing analysis. *The Columbian*, pp. D1, D7.

Prather, H. (1970). *Notes to myself.* Moab, UT: Real People Press.

Prelle, C. (2006). *No laughing matter: How gender affects the use and appreciation of humor.* Unpublished senior honors thesis, Duke University, Durham, NC.

Parmar, N. (1995). Therapy: The laugh track. *Psychology Today, 38(1)*, 35.

Ronne, N. (1998). *The use of humor in psychoanalysis.* Retrieved March 29, 2006, from http://www.4therapy.com/consumer/life_topics/article/7250/489/The+Use+of+Humor+in+Psychoanalysis

Segal, J., Jaffe, J., DeKoven, G., & DeKoven, B. (last revised May 8, 2006) Part Two: Becoming a Pro. eBook.

Shepell, W. (2006). *Lighten up: Humour in the workplace.* Retrieved August 28, 2006, from http://www.warrenshepell.com/articles/humour.asp

Sloshberg, S. K. (1996). *Counselor perceptions of humor within the counseling context.* Unpublished doctoral dissertation, University of Connecticut, Storrs, CT.

Snyer, L. M., & Cabianca, W. A. (1972). *An experiential approach to interview training.* Tempe, AZ: Heuristic Systems.

Stambor, Z. (2006). The chuckle connection. *Monitor on Psychology, 37(6)*, 60–61.

Stambor, Z. (2006). How laughing leads to learning. *Monitor on Psychology*,
   37(6), 62–64.
Sultanoff, S. (1993). *Taking humor seriously in the workplace.* Retrieved April
   26, 2006, from http://humormatters.com/articles/workplace.htm
Sultanoff, S. (1999, Fall). President's Column. *Association for Applied and Therapeutic Humor Newsletter, XIII*(3), 3.
Toosi, N. (2006, August 29). Loud and weird: Overheard site is the talk of N.Y.
   The Seattle Times, p. A2.
Toupin, E. B. (2006). *Career know-how: A sense of humor in the workplace is it
   me? Or, was that not funny?* Retrieved August 28, 2006, from
   http://www.careerknowhow.com/guidance/humor.htm
Vereen, L. G., Butler, S. K., Williams, F. C., Darg, J. A., & Downing T. K. E.
   (2006). The use of humor when counseling African American college stu-
   dents. *Journal of Counseling & Development, 84*(1), 10–15.
Wanzer (1999). *Communication Education 48*(1), 48–62.
Wilson, G. D. (1999). Personality and individual differences. In W. D. Ruch
   (Ed.), *The sense of humor: Explorations of a personality characteristic* (pp.
   1146–1147). London, England: Institute of Psychiatry, University of London. Retrieved April 26, 2006 on http://www.uni-dusseldorf.de
Yonkovitz, E., & Matthews, W. (1998). The strategic uses of humor in psychotherapy. *Journal of Systemic Therapies, 17*(3), 45–69.

Index

A

Absurdity, 1, 2, 4, 5, 6, 42, 47, 74, 75, 79, 80
Applications of humor
  in counseling, 7, 74–78
  in illness, 7, 61–64
  in long-distance parent-child relationships, 7, 64–67
  in professional settings, 19–20, 24–25
  in religious settings, 25–26
  in wartime, 7, 67–68

B

Barriers to humor, 6, 23–31, 80
  cultural expectations. *See* Cultural considerations
  fear of appearing foolish, 27
  fear of appearing unprofessional, 24–26
  fear of not being seen as serious, 27
  fear of others' response, 26–27
  gender norms, 27–28. *See also* Gender differences, Gender socialization
  view of self as lacking humor, 23–24
Benefits of humor, 5–6, 9–22, 63–64, 72, 73, 74, 75, 80

physical, 5, 9–10, 16–18, 22, 79, 80
psychological, 5, 9, 10, 18–22, 80
social, 6, 9, 10–15, 22

C

Cartoons, 15, 21, 28, 29, 54, 62, 63, 67, 71, 73, 78, 83
Constructive humor, 5, 6, 12, 29–31, 39
Cultural considerations, 6, 21, 27–28, 57, 71, 74, 77, 78, 80
Cynicism, 73

D

Destructive humor, 6, 12, 29–31, 39
Disparaging humor, 42, 72, 74

E

Endorphin, 9, 16
Expectations for being funny, 28–29

F

Fear of offending, 29
Female humor, 28

Metaphorical stems, 58
Mirthmyopia, 5

N

Negative humor. *See* Destructive
  humor

O

Obstacles to humor. *See* Barriers to
  humor

P

Playfulness, 2, 17, 19, 40, 41, 43
Positive humor. *See* Constructive
  humor
Puns, 7, 47, 51–54
Pun wheel, 52

R

Referential in–jokes, 13–14
  wartime,

S

Sarcasm, 14, 29, 42
Safe humor rules, 72, 73
Satire, 15, 29

Self-disparaging humor, 28, 72, 74,
  80. *See also* Laughing at oneself
Self esteem, 29
Similes, 47, 57
Stages of relationships, 40
  caring, 41–42
  conflict, 42–43
  deeper level of caring, 43–44
  final parting, 43, 44–45
  getting acquainted, 40–41

meeting, 40
reconciliation, 43
separation, 43

T

Teasing, 31, 41, 43
Teleworker, 74
Timing, 26, 27, 29, 61, 75, 77

V

Verbal caricatures, 7, 54–57
Virtual teams, 7, 71, 74

W

Wartime,
Workplace humor, 7, 19–20, 71–73

Made in United States
North Haven, CT
13 February 2024

48689146R00075